KAMALA ~~~~~~
THE AMERICAN STORY THAT BEGAN
ON INDIA'S SHORES

Hansa Makhijani Jain juggles her time between writing and editing. In the 14 years that she has been in media, she has written prolifically across newspapers, magazines, books and the web. She served as assistant editor at *Marie Claire India*, and regularly contributed to magazines such as *Harper's Bazaar*, *Cosmopolitan*, *L'Officiel*, *eShe* and *Prevention*. She has also been deputy editor at Fashion101. in, a property of Dainik Bhaskar Digital, is the co-author of *Your Happy Pregnancy Handbook* and has written four introductory volumes on orthopaedics. She currently works as a freelancer.

KAMALA HARRIS

THE AMERICAN STORY THAT BEGAN ON INDIA'S SHORES

HANSA MAKHIJANI JAIN

First published in 2021 by Hachette India
(Registered name: Hachette Book Publishing India Pvt. Ltd)
An Hachette UK company
www.hachetteindia.com

1

ISBN 978-81-946577-9-8

Hachette Book Publishing India Pvt. Ltd
4th & 5th Floors, Corporate Centre,
Plot No. 94, Sector 44, Gurugram 122003, India

Typeset in Adobe Garamond Pro 11.5/16
by R. Ajith Kumar, New Delhi

MIX
Paper from
responsible sources
FSC® C010615

Printed and bound in India
by Thomson Press India Ltd.

'I have my own legacy.'

— KAMALA HARRIS

CONTENTS

PROLOGUE

WHETHER IT IS DURING HER CAMPAIGN TRAIL OR in her victory speech after being elected vice president of the United States of America, the one person Kamala Devi Harris has quoted most often is her mother. Before her death in 2009, Shyamala Gopalan Harris, mother and role model to Kamala and her sister Maya, had made sure she had raised gutsy girls who were motivated and driven to make a difference in the world.

When Kamala was twelve and Maya nine, Shyamala, a single mother by then, accepted a research and teaching position at the McGill University-affiliated Jewish General Hospital in the Canadian city of Montreal in Quebec. According to a feature in the *Washington Post*, 'The Harris sisters remember the Mayflower truck coming to bring all their belongings across the continent, they remember arriving at their apartment and hiding from the cold in the closet, and they remember how their relationship further solidified in a place where no one else spoke their language.'

At the age of thirteen, as her sister Maya recalls in an interview to *San Francisco Gate*, Kamala organized a protest in front of the building in which they resided. She managed to rope in her peers to join the demonstration against the owner who had prohibited children from playing on the lawns. Standing up for what she thought was right came naturally to Kamala, as she had witnessed several demonstrations since her infancy, her parents having participated in some protest or the other. In this instance, Kamala and her cohort ultimately persuaded the owner to scrap the rule. That was her first call to justice – and it was just the beginning.

In Montreal, Kamala was first enrolled in the Notre-Dame-des-Neiges School, where the first language was French. Having lived in America for most of her life until then, Kamala admitted to her mother that she was having trouble coping with the new language she had just been introduced to. For a brief period after that she went to F.A.C.E. School in Montreal, before being admitted to Westmount High School in Westmount, Quebec, from where she graduated in 1981. At Westmount High School, Kamala befriended Wanda Kagan and the two became inseparable. The girls formed a dance troupe by the name of Midnight Magic and performed at community centres for elderly folk and sometimes at fundraisers.

But something was happening in Kagan's life that her best friend was unaware of.

'When I was in high school I was being molested by my stepfather. Kamala and I were best friends and I [eventually] shared the information with her, which is not always easy to do,' Kagan told CBC News in an interview after her friend's big win. When Kamala told her mother about what her friend was going through, Shyamala insisted Kagan come and stay with them at once, at least till their graduation. Without a second thought, Shyamala made a commitment to end the young girl's suffering.

'I stayed with them for the latter part of the high school year… Her mom helped me navigate through different things with the system,' Kagan said. 'Her sister Maya [too] was wonderful… Kamala is who she is [and] a large part of her mom. [Her mother] was short, four-foot-something but she was a strong, strong, independent woman.'

In one night, without sitting them down for a life lesson, Shyamala Gopalan Harris had taught her daughters about justice, equality, kindness and standing up for the rights of others. She led by example. Through an instantaneous gesture, she had categorically conveyed that one should do whatever one can, even within limited means, to pull a person in need out of a crisis. This incident, etched forever in Kamala's consciousness, was just one of the many little things that would set the course for the rest of her life.

1

MAMA'S GIRL

'My mother, Shyamala Gopalan Harris, was a force of nature and the greatest source of inspiration in my life. She taught my sister Maya and me the importance of hard work and to believe in our power to right what is wrong.'

– Kamala Harris, in a tweet on the occasion of
Women's History Month

ALTHOUGH, AT JUST AROUND FIVE FEET, SHYAMALA Gopalan Harris was not a physically imposing figure, her presence was immense. Born in the Madras Presidency, British India, in 1940, she was the eldest of the four children of senior civil servant Painganadu Venkataraman Gopalan, whom she admired deeply.

Being born into a family of politically conscious high achievers meant that Shyamala would never be discouraged from pursuing her passions. Her life would not be restricted to domestic activities like cooking and sewing, as was the lot of other girls of her generation. Owing to the nature of her father's job, Shyamala grew up in major cities in British and independent India such as Delhi, Bombay, Madras and Calcutta. She earned her bachelor's degree in home science from Lady Irwin College in Delhi. Although her first choice was biochemistry, she was forced to study home science due to the college's internal rules. Her parents believed the subject did not do justice to her abilities, and her brother and father, who knew that her heart was really in biochemistry, would often joke with her about her having to learn how to set a table as part of her home science curriculum. Shyamala took it all as friendly banter but she did not give up on her dream. After her graduation, Shyamala secretly applied to the University of California, Berkeley, one of the most renowned land grant universities in the United States. She broke the news to her family only when she was accepted. With her father's blessings, in 1959, at the age of nineteen, Shyamala travelled to Berkeley. Little did she know that she would continue to stay on in her adopted country and call it home for the rest of her days.

'At the time, there were not many Indians living in the Bay Area. And certainly no single girls,' Shyamala's brother Gopalan Balachandran, who lives in Delhi, told *NBC News* in an interview. 'She did a lot of things which...very few had done at the time. And she did them of her own volition because of what she believed in.' Her father had agreed to pay her tuition fee only for a year. After that she would be on her own. It was clear that Gopalan wanted his children to be independent and chart the course of their lives, and it is this spirit that Balachandran claimed his sister had passed down to her daughters. In due course, Balachandran would also land in the United States to study, earning his doctorate in economics and computer science from the University of Wisconsin and eventually returning to work in his own country.

Shyamala went on to receive her Ph.D. in nutrition and endocrinology, and made significant and pivotal contributions to breast cancer research. She is specifically well known for her work on progesterone receptor biology and its applications in breast cancer.

Shyamala first met Donald Jasper Harris in the fall of 1962 at a meeting of black students. The young graduate student from Jamaica was then studying to become an economist and was the speaker at the gathering. To him, the traditional sari-clad

Shyamala immediately stood out among the herd of students. He could not take his eyes off her. She approached him after his address, and thus began their acquaintance. In the months to come, they would bond over a shared passion for the Civil Rights Movement, which was the mainstay of campus life. They decided to tie the knot in 1963, a bold step for an Indian, particularly for a Tamil Brahmin girl to marry an African rather than choose the 'safe' option of a match arranged by her family within the same community. There was almost nothing in common between them – apart from being born in countries colonized by the British. They married without following the conventions of their families being introduced to each other or indulging in a traditional Indian wedding ceremony at Shyamala's native village. In due course they had two daughters – Kamala Devi Harris, born on 20 October 1964, and her sister, Maya Lakshmi Harris, born on 30 January 1966.

The environment at the Harris home, much like in Shyamala's home in India, was always politically charged. 'From both of my grandparents, my mother developed a keen political consciousness. She was conscious of history, conscious of struggle, conscious of inequities. She was born with a sense of justice imprinted on her soul,' Kamala writes in her memoir, *The Truths We Hold: An American Journey.*

Even when Kamala was barely two weeks old, her parents were engrossed in watching election results rather than cooing away to the newborn and making diaper runs. And who could blame them? The evening of 3 November 1964 marked a meaningful change in California's history – it was the first time in sixteen years that a Democrat swept the state. President Lyndon Johnson triumphed over Senator Barry Goldwater, the Arizona Republican, bagging nearly 60 per cent of California's vote and thus obtaining a mandate that for a while would assist him in expanding his domestic policy of the Great Society and civil rights. Frequent political discussions became the constant Kamala and her sister were exposed to from their infancy.

From Berkeley to the University of Illinois in Champaign-Urbana (where Maya was born) to Northwestern University in Evanston and the University of Wisconsin in Madison, Donald was always hopscotching from one city to another in the early years of his career. However, this was the era of transformative politics and during the time Shyamala and Donald Harris lived together in Berkeley and Oakland, it was the epicentre of the Free Speech Movement. The rise of environmentalism and demands for racial justice were beginning to take root, and the girls attended protests with their parents right from their toddler years.

In her memoir, Kamala recalls listening to her parents' music collections. While Shyamala, a gifted singer herself, enjoyed humming along to Gospel music, Donald had a fine taste in jazz. Shyamala adopted her husband's religion by becoming a Protestant Christian, while continuing to visit Hindu temples and occasionally singing devotional songs there. This exposed the girls not only to a biracial and bicultural but also an inter-faith way of life. It is this background that Kamala Harris's appeal is credited to, cutting across many American identities. As a report on BBC.com stated, 'Those parts of the country which have seen rapid demographic change, enough change to alter a region's politics, see an aspirational symbol in her.'

Unfortunately, with Shyamala and Donald separating in 1969, the girls had to deal with emotional upheaval very early in life. At the time Kamala was five and Maya, three. The couple finally filed for divorce in January 1972, while Donald was employed at the University of Wisconsin. 'I knew they loved each other very much, but it seemed like they had become like oil and water,' writes Kamala in her memoir. While Shyamala got physical custody of the girls, Donald was permitted to see them on every other weekend and for sixty days in the summer. In the same year, Donald joined the faculty at Stanford University, where he went on to become the first black economist to achieve tenure in the economics department. He visited India at this time as a visiting fellow at the Delhi School of Economics. He was also a visiting professor at Yale University. Ironically, even though he has written that he had no great desire to be at Stanford, he stayed on at the university, where he holds the status of professor emeritus, until his retirement in 1998. Recalling the time, Kamala writes in her memoir, 'My father remained a part of our lives. We would see him on weekends and spend summers with him in Palo Alto. But it was really my mother who took charge of our upbringing. She was the one most responsible for shaping us into the women we would become.'

Roughly a year after the separation, Shyamala

moved into the top floor of a duplex on Bancroft Way with the girls. This part of Berkeley, known as Flatlands, was populated by working-class families and Kamala recalls it as a close-knit neighbourhood – a community in which everyone had each other's backs. 'We weren't rich in financial terms, but the values we internalized provided a different kind of wealth. My mom would get Maya and me ready every morning before heading to work at her research lab,' she writes in *The Truths We Hold*. They came to be an inseparable trio and would often be referred to as a unit – people spoke of them as 'Shyamala and the girls'. About the relationship she shared with her mother and younger sister, especially since the time it was just the three of them, Kamala told the *Washington Post*, 'We forged a bond that is unbreakable. When I think about it, all of the joyous moments in our lives, all of the challenging moments, all of the moments of transition, we have always been together.'

Kamala has mentioned several times in interviews that she can sometimes be a snob about food as her mother would prepare everything from scratch. Despite being a single working mother, Shyamala took no shortcuts. When she appeared on a show with Mindy Kaling for her YouTube channel in October 2020 and was praised for her 'fine' onion chopping skills, Kamala admitted it was one of the skills she had picked up from her mother, having spent valuable time in the kitchen with Shyamala when she was growing up. Kamala is known to be quite a foodie and has been seen on numerous cookery shows, though, as she admits herself, her favourite food has always been her mother's daal, dosa, potato curry and idli.

Maya Harris, Kamala's sister and a well-known civil rights lawyer, also credits her parents' involvement in activism for her choice of career. 'Their activism and what they were striving to achieve was what we talked about at the dinner table,' she says in an article published in her law school's magazine. 'I knew at a very early age that I was going to one day have a career that would allow me to work for social justice and focus on improving the quality of people's lives.'

After receiving her Bachelor of Arts degree from the University of California, Berkeley, in 1989, she went on to join Stanford Law School. She had her only child, a daughter, Meena Harris, when she was seventeen. But even with all the responsibilities of a young single mother, she continued to study. Shyamala would help by babysitting little Meena so that Maya could finish her college education. In 1992, she left Stanford after receiving her Juris Doctor degree with distinction. It was also at Stanford that she became friends with her future husband, Tony West, though they started dating after graduation. They married in 1998, nearly a decade after they first met. West has served former President Barack Obama as assistant attorney general in the Department of Justice, Civil Division. An award-winning lawyer herself, Maya has often been called the 'next Bobby Kennedy' and she played significant roles in the presidential campaigns of Hillary Clinton in 2016 and sister Kamala in 2019.

Like her sister, Maya too acknowledges their mother's significant influence on their lives and careers. In an article in the Spring 2010 issue of Stanford Law School's magazine, Maya wrote, 'She [my mother] was accomplished in her field, yet always the activist helping others, whether women who were disproportionately impacted by breast cancer or students trying to get financial aid. Her example and her core values made a very deep impression on me, and my sister.'

The sisters, who do not look much like each other, with Kamala resembling their father and Maya's features more like their mother's, have always been very close. At Kamala Harris's swearing-in ceremony for the post of attorney general in 2014, it was Maya who held the Bible. 'I think most people who know Maya will tell you she's one of the smartest people they know,' Kamala said while speaking to *Politico* about her sister's involvement in her election campaign in 2020. 'The fact that she has volunteered to work on this campaign at such a high level and she's exactly who she's always been – she works around the clock and she's probably the hardest, if not one of the hardest working people on the campaign – I feel very blessed.'

Away from the public eye, Maya had been fighting a battle of her own for a long time. When she was 22, just on the brink of starting law school, she was diagnosed with the autoimmune disease lupus. In an interview with *Women's Health* magazine, she talked about her experience of dealing with it, with a four-year-old daughter in tow. 'Countless times my mother had told me I could do anything I put my mind to, no matter the obstacles I might encounter. "Don't dwell on it, hold your head up, summon the strength to move through it and emerge on the other side,"' she recalls her mother telling her. During the despairing times of the pandemic, Maya felt the need to reveal the secret that only a handful of people had known for three decades.

Meanwhile, ironically, their cancer researcher mother was diagnosed with colon cancer. Shyamala, who was ferried to chemotherapy sessions by both her daughters, had begun to lose interest in most things that had once fascinated her – including political developments and the news. In a *New York Times* op-ed, Kamala wrote about telling her mother of her decision to run for the post of attorney general, the election for which would take place two years later and the tough competition she anticipated facing. '"Mommy, these guys are saying they're going to kick my ass," I told her.' Shyamala said nothing and just rolled over to beam the brightest smile at her daughter. 'She knew who she'd raised. She knew her fighting spirit was alive and well inside me,' wrote Kamala.

On 11 February 2009, Shyamala Gopalan Harris bid adieu to her daughters as she succumbed to colon cancer in Oakland. In 2020, when Kamala broke through the world's highest glass ceiling by being elected vice president of the United States of America, Maya posted an emotional tweet, saying, 'Mommy taught us we could be and do anything. She would be beyond proud today.'

Not a week goes by where Kamala does not recount inspiring anecdotes about her mother while discussing matters with the people she works with closely. One of her mother's favourite nuggets of wisdom, which Kamala has often reiterated in public as well, is intrinsically ingrained in her: 'You may be the first to do many things, but make sure you are not the last.'

2

HALF-INDIAN,
HALF-JAMAICAN,
FULLY AMERICAN

'My parents would bring me to protests strapped tightly in my stroller, and my mother, Shyamala, raised my sister, Maya, and me to believe that it was up to us and every generation of Americans to keep on marching.'

– **Kamala Harris**, during her first campaign appearance as the Democratic Party nominee for vice president of the United States of America

DESPITE HER AMERICAN UPBRINGING, KAMALA HAS
always been in close touch with her roots. Kamala
and Maya's father, Donald J. Harris, who came to
America on a scholarship sponsored by the colonial
Jamaican government in the fall of 1961, would
arrange for frequent visits for the sisters to Jamaica
to meet with relatives and give them a peek into
his childhood. Being an economist and a renowned
professor, it was extremely important for him to
expose the girls to an alternative reality to the one
they lived and witnessed in the United States. In
an essay titled 'Reflections of a Jamaican Father'
published on Jamaica Global, he wrote, 'I would
also try to explain to them the contradictions of
economic and social life in a "poor" country, like
the striking juxtaposition of extreme poverty and

extreme wealth, while working hard myself with the government of Jamaica to design a plan and appropriate policies to do something about those conditions.'

The Stanford professor emeritus, now in his eighties, also recalls in the essay one of his fondest memories with his daughters Kamala and Maya in Jamaica from a time before the custody battle ensued, after which there was a decline in the intimacy and closeness they had shared. Etched in his memory is a visit they made to Orange Hill in 1970. 'We trudged through the cow dung and rusted iron gates, uphill and downhill, along narrow unkempt paths, to the very end of the family property, all in my eagerness to show to the girls the terrain over which I had wandered daily for hours as a boy.' He continues, 'Upon reaching the top of a little hill that opened much of that terrain to our full view, Kamala, ever the adventurous and assertive one, suddenly broke from the pack, leaving behind Maya the more cautious one, and took off like a gazelle in Serengeti, leaping over rocks and shrubs and fallen branches, in utter joy and unleashed curiosity, to explore that same enticing terrain. I quickly followed her with my trusted Canon Super

Eight movie camera to record the moment (in my usual role as cameraman for every occasion). I couldn't help thinking there and then: What a moment of exciting rediscovery being handed over from one generation to another!'

Over the years, Donald has been part of his daughters' lives. He has also described the joy he felt holding his great-granddaughter (Maya's granddaughter) in his lap and feeling the same emotions that his grandmother, Miss Iris, may have felt on holding Kamala for the first time.

Kamala's extended family in India, whom she has visited more frequently than she has her father's clan, has always been proud of Kamala's feats. Her maternal uncle, Gopalan Balachandran, who now lives in Delhi, voiced his jubilation on his niece's vice presidential nomination, saying he was not at all surprised by it. Though separated by miles, the family had kept a close watch on the landmarks in Kamala's luminous career and admired her for her tenacity and spirit. Balachandran admitted that his phone had not stopped ringing since his niece joined the vice presidential race in the United States. 'Having studied US policy and politics for many years, I knew Kamala was the perfect candidate. The only thing I felt is, why did it take them so long to decide?' he told ThePrint.in. 'Due to the Black Lives Matter movement, the African American community was looking for key representation. Her credentials as a district attorney and senator, too, were important, along with the fact that she's a woman.'

When Kamala finally won, the elation was particularly high in Thulasendrapuram, her ancestral village in Tamil Nadu. According to a report in *The Hindu*, residents of the village took the celebration to the streets, holding up her posters, bursting firecrackers and distributing sweets to express their joy. Once home to Kamala's maternal grandfather, P.V. Gopalan, Thulasendrapuram is a sparsely populated village in the district of Tiruvarur. 'Villagers woke up early in the day and drew colourful kolams with captions in front of their homes hailing the victory of Ms Harris. "Congratulations Kamala Harris – The Pride of Our Village" read a caption drawn along with a colourful kolam in front of one of the houses at Thulasendrapuram,' stated *The Hindu* report.

There were similar outpourings of delight in Jamaica. A news article in the *Washington Post* revealed that Jamaica's prime minister, Andrew Holness, saluted Harris's 'monumental accomplishment for women' as well as her Jamaican heritage. 'To have one of our own reach one of the highest seats on the world stage is humbling and profound,' said Latoya Harris, 39, a policy analyst in Jamaica and Kamala's second cousin.

Kamala and Maya had always been particularly close to their two aunts and enjoyed their support at every turn. Their chitti (that is, their mother's younger sister), Dr Sarala Gopalan, based in Tamil Nadu's Chennai, remembers breaking coconuts at the temple on Kamala's request to pray for her while she was running for the post of the attorney general of California. When Kamala was on the campaign trail, she followed the same ritual, this time without being asked. 'I did break 108 coconuts, but without her asking me to do so,' she told Rediff.com in an interview. 'She didn't even know that I did [that]. As attorney general, she did very well and coped up with the work. She fought to get many things done for the state of California and that is why she won [the US Senate race] by such a huge margin… After she decided to run for the Senate and before she filed the nomination, she called all of us, her aunts and uncle, and told us of her decision. We hoped for the best as we wanted the best for her. She really wanted to achieve this,' she said.

Dr Gopalan also talked about the immeasurable contribution that Kamala's mother had made towards shaping Kamala's personality. Shyamala ensured that her daughters visited Chennai often and introduced them to Hindu temples and mythology. 'Even though she [Kamala] was born and brought up in America, my sister inculcated in her South Indian culture and values. She believes in going to the temple because her mother believed in it. Kamala is what she is today because of her mother. The credit doesn't go to any other person. It is my sister, her mother, who brought her up like this,' she said.

Kamala's youngest maternal aunt, Mahalakshmi, who is based in Canada, flew in to be by Kamala's side during the campaign. After Shyamala's demise, Mahalakshmi has been especially proactive, taking a keen interest in her nieces' lives and well-being. During the campaign Mahalakshmi travelled extensively with Kamala, attending rallies and other gatherings. Apart from keeping the family posted on the details of the campaign, she also whipped up delectable South Indian fare for Kamala and her husband.

According to certain news reports, a segment of Indian Americans grumble about Kamala giving more importance to her African identity over her Indian one. Kamala's rationale for this is that when their mother realized that in her adopted country her daughters would be seen as 'black girls', she raised them as 'black daughters'. More so because they bore their father's last name – they were Kamala and Maya Harris, not Gopalan. Yet, there is no denying that Kamala shares a much closer bond with her mother's side of the family.

However the media projects her, Kamala has often said that she is proud of her identity. She has also emphatically expressed her opinion that politicians should not have to fit into compartments because of their colour or background. As she told the *Washington Post* in 2019, 'My point was: I am who I am. I'm good with it. You might need to figure it out, but I'm fine with it.'

3

STARTING YOUNG

'One of my mother's favorite sayings was, "Don't let anybody tell you who you are. You tell them who you are." And so I did. I knew part of making change was what I'd seen all my life, surrounded by adults shouting and marching and demanding justice from the outside. But I also knew there was an important role on the inside, sitting at the table where the decisions were being made. When activists came marching and banging on the doors, I wanted to be on the other side to let them in.'

– **Kamala Harris**, *The Truths We Hold:*
An American Journey

WHEN KAMALA BEGAN HER ELEMENTARY EDUCATION in Oakland, Alameda County, California, schools in the United States were still in the process of being desegregated. The schooling system, much like everything else in America of the 1960s and 1970s, was rife with racism and separate schools for whites and blacks were the norm. In fact, the integration of schools was a matter of great importance during the Civil Rights Movement and in 1971 the Supreme Court approved the use of bussing to practically implement and promote desegregation. Like other students of colour at the time, Kamala too would witness the surge in school integration and benefit from the bussing scheme. Among the second batch of students to experience segregation, she rode the bus to a wealthier, prosperous, whiter neighbourhood to attend Thousand Oaks Elementary School, Northern Berkeley, Alameda County, roughly fifteen minutes from her home. School integration reached its peak around 1988 with over 40 per cent black students studying in schools that were earlier categorized as all-white.

However, while the government had allowed mixed-race schools on paper, deep-seated attitudes of discrimination were harder to get rid of on the ground. Segregationist politicians such as Senators James O. Eastland of Mississippi and Herman E. Talmadge of Georgia made efforts to block bussing to prevent desegregation of public schools. The idea of their wards being educated in a mixed-race environment was repulsive to many in the white community and parents of white children began to demand, sometimes vehemently, that their children's schools not admit people of colour.

Growing up in a politically aware household, Kamala, then a young student, observed everything in her changing milieu. Experiencing these vicissitudes first-hand instilled in her a keen interest in political developments and dialogues around racism and inclusion from a tender age, and helped her to find her feet, from her very first day, at Howard

University in Washington, DC, the historically black institution in the American capital. She had enrolled there to study political science and economics after graduating from high school in Montreal. The campus, perched on a hilltop in Northwest Washington, is a stone's throw from the National Mall where Kamala would be found with her friends on weekends protesting against the apartheid regime in South Africa. Kamala's time at Howard fuelled her political and social consciousness further and influenced her deeply. She found the diversity on the campus exhilarating. In her memoir, Kamala describes with passion what it meant to her to be a student at Howard. 'Every signal told students that we could be anything – that we were young, gifted, and black, and we shouldn't let anything get in the way of our success. The campus was a place where you didn't have to be confined to the box of another person's choosing… We weren't just told we had the capacity to be great; we were challenged to live up to that potential. There was an expectation that we would cultivate and use our talents to take on roles of leadership and have an impact on other people, on our country, and maybe even on the world.'

In an interview with the *Washington Post*, Kamala proclaimed, 'I became an adult at Howard University. Howard very directly influenced and reinforced – equally important – my sense of being and meaning and reasons for being.'

The university would also serve as the place that offered the future vice president of America her first taste of politics. In her freshman year, she ran for her first elected office: freshman class representative of the Liberal Arts Student Council. 'It was my very first campaign. No opponent I've faced since was as tough as Jersey Girl Shelley Young...' Kamala mentions in her memoir. In 1986, Kamala graduated from Howard University and got a chance to intern in the office of California Senator Alan Cranston.

Kamala went on to study at the University of California Hastings College of the Law. Having earned her Juris Doctor degree in 1989, she chose to pursue a legal career influenced, in part, by her maternal grandfather, P.V. Gopalan. In the introduction to her book, *Smart on Crime: A Career Prosecutor's Plan to Make Us Safer*, Kamala writes fondly of her visits to India every two years and the indelible mark they left on her, and refers particularly to her grandfather's influence on her life. 'My grandfather would talk to me about the importance of doing the right thing, the just thing. He was part of the movement for India to gain independence, and later became Joint Secretary for the Indian government, a post akin to our [United States's] Deputy Secretary of State. He had numerous foreign service assignments, including several years as an advisor to the newly independent government of Zambia in Africa... My grandmother was betrothed to him at age twelve and began living with him at sixteen, and she was quite a force in her own right. After they were married, she would sometimes take to the streets with a bullhorn to talk to poor women about how they could get birth control.' During the time spent in India in her childhood and youth, she often overheard her grandfather talking to his friends on their walks on the beach. Their conversations on politics, corruption and justice fascinated her. 'Lawyers have a profound ability and responsibility to be a voice for the vulnerable and the voiceless,' she said on her decision to opt for a career in law in an interview published in the Spring 2013 issue of her law school's magazine. During her years at

Hastings, she held the post of president of the Black Law Students Association and was also a part of the Legal Education Opportunity Program at which she would advocate with great fervour for more diversity on their campus.

Interestingly, Kamala failed the bar exam on her first attempt. Not that this in any way disheartened her. She had after all joined the ranks of other prominent icons, such as Michelle Obama and John F. Kennedy, Jr., who built successful careers for themselves after failing the same exam on the initial try. Once she cracked the bar exam in June 1990, there was no stopping her. She went on to become the first African American, the first South Asian and the first woman to hold the post of district attorney of San Francisco. However, like every other rookie fresh from passing the bar exam, she started out handling cases of misdemeanours such as drunk driving and preliminary procedural stages of felony. In the next year and a half Kamala served at branch courthouses in Fremont, Hayward, before returning to work at the Wiley Manuel Courthouse in Oakland.

One of the most talked-about cases during Kamala's early years of practising law was that of

American lawyer and academic Anita Faye Hill's accusation of sexual harassment against Judge Clarence Thomas in Washington in October 1991. Thomas, who was at the time serving at the United States Court of Appeals for the District of Columbia Circuit, had been nominated to the Supreme Court of the United States by then President George W. Bush to replace Thurgood Marshall, the civil rights icon who had recently announced his retirement. Although Thomas's nomination attracted much criticism on account of his relative lack of experience and conservative views, the confirmation hearings in the Senate proceeded without much disruption. Then US Senator Joseph Biden was chairman of the Senate Judiciary Committee during these hearings.

Even as the committee entered the final phase of discussion before approving the nomination, a leaked Federal Bureau of Investigations (FBI) report brought to light University of Oklahoma law school professor Hill's allegations of sexual impropriety against Clarence Thomas. In the televised hearings that followed, Hill testified that Thomas had sexually harassed her while he was her supervisor at the Department of Education and later at the Equal Employment Opportunity Commission, pressuring her for dates, making lewd remarks and talking about X-rated films. While Thomas denied the charges, the Senate Judiciary Committee was seen as trivializing the allegations made by Hill and Biden was criticized for his role as chairman of the committee, first for not postponing the scheduled vote by the Senators until he was pressured to do so and in general for the way in which the hearings were conducted in spite of the allegations. Eventually, Thomas's nomination was confirmed, and he was sworn in as an associate justice of the Supreme Court on 23 October 1991, much to the dismay of women's rights activists and those who had opposed Thomas's nomination to begin with. The case and its outcome deeply impacted young female lawyers like Kamala who would go on to take a keen interest in addressing gender-related violence and prejudices within and outside the system.

The next phase of Kamala's career – when, in 1992, she ventured into an assignment to work in juvenile court – proved to be an intense learning experience for the young lawyer. In this job, Kamala oversaw many cases of violence, abuse and sexual exploitation. The cases she handled are known to have made a great impact on her. During this time she also witnessed the makings of a major issue that was heatedly debated during the United States presidential election in 2020 – the tension between the African American community and law enforcement, and the disproportion in the number of arrests and cases of imprisonment of black citizens in the country. When Kamala began working in the juvenile court in California in the 1990s, there flourished a political culture that was happy to take a tough-on-crime stance, and the black community was hit hardest. While similar laws to apprehend criminals were being passed across the country, California gained attention for enacting some of the strictest measures. It brought into practice a 'three strikes and you're out' policy, which saw the state's prison population surge. Having witnessed all the strife, Kamala decided she would run for elective office in the hope of bringing about change in the community.

'When I realized that I wanted to work in the district attorney's office – that I had found my calling – I was excited to share the decision with my friends and family,' Kamala writes in her memoir. 'And I wasn't surprised to find them incredulous. I had to defend my choice as one would a thesis.'

Her family knew she was driven to work for the welfare of women and children, to fight for justice for those who did not have adequate representation and be a voice for the voiceless, but elective office was a different ballgame altogether. The family had thought she would help bring about justice from outside the system as a prosecutor, but it now seemed she wanted to work her way from the inside out.

4

BODY OF WORK

'As I left the Supreme Court, there were hundreds of people gathered, waving rainbow flags, holding signs, waiting anxiously for justice. It made me smile. They were why I had become a lawyer in the first place. It was in the courtroom, I believed, that you could translate that passion into action and precedent and law.'

– **Kamala Harris**, *The Truths We Hold:*
An American Journey

THROUGHOUT HER CAREER, KAMALA HAS ADVOCATED
on various key societal issues that have not only
accelerated her dreams and ambitions, and got her
noticed, but also affected countless lives.

During the week of Valentine's Day, in 2004,
Gavin Newsom, who was serving as San Francisco's
mayor at the time, decided to allow marriage for
same-sex couples in the state. Four years later, the
people of California voted in favour of Proposition 8,
prohibiting same-sex marriages in California and
leaving a whole community disheartened and in
the lurch. This was the same night that Barack
Obama was elected President of the United States
in 2008. Since it was a constitutional amendment,
the law came into force with immediate effect –
from the moment its enactment was announced

no wedding ceremonies could take place between same-sex couples in the state of California. The situation was particularly trying for couples who were already married. The law no longer recognized their union, and in effect the lives they had built together no longer meant anything.

However, all was not lost. The doors of the federal courts could still be knocked on. The American Foundation for Equal Rights, founded by political strategist Chad Griffin and led by him at the time, decided that the solution to the problem lay in bringing a suit against the State of California. The foundation's case was based on their view that Proposition 8 dishonoured the protections granted to all citizens in the Fourteenth Amendment to the American Constitution, that is, equal protection and due process in the eyes of the law.

Ruling in favour of the foundation's petition on 4 August 2010, Chief Judge Vaughn Walker concluded that Proposition 8 was unconstitutional. Although the ruling would only be enforced until it was appealed in a higher court, for the present same-sex marriages were legal in California again.

'I was in the middle of my race for attorney general when the ruling came down, and it quickly became a central issue in the campaign. The California attorney general had the right to appeal the decision. Jerry Brown, whom I was running to succeed, had refused to defend the measure in court. I, too, made clear that I had no intention of spending a penny of the attorney general's office's resources defending Prop 8,' Kamala says in her memoir. Kamala's opponent, however, took the other view. It became clear to her, she wrote, that it 'wasn't just about principle; it was about practical outcomes'. If there was no appeal against the ruling, the stay on same-sex marriages could be lifted and marriage licences issued again, with immediate effect. But if there was an appeal, it would take years for the matter to be resolved and for same-sex marriages to become legal in the state again. Later in 2010, Kamala became the thirty-second attorney general of California (she was eventually sworn in on 3 January 2011).

The hearings on Proposition 8 were intense as its specifics were discussed in great depth. 'As I sat listening to the oral arguments, the Supreme Court justices homed in on the issue of standing. Justice Stephen Breyer questioned whether the Prop 8 proponents were "no more than a group of five people who feel really strongly". Justice Sonia Sotomayor wanted to know how the lower court's ruling had caused the proponents an injury "separate from that of every other taxpayer to have laws enforced".' But when the arguments were over, there was really no way to tell what the decision would be. Finally, on 26 June 2013, the Supreme Court dismissed the case, validating the lower court's ruling. Justice had finally been served. Within hours of the decision, plaintiffs in the Supreme Court case Kris Perry and Sandy Stier announced their wedding. They were the first gay couple to tie the knot in San Francisco, and it was Kamala Harris, by then attorney general of California, who officiated at their wedding, held at the San Francisco City Hall.

Kamala Harris's fighting spirit was evident from the time she was elected district attorney of San Francisco, a post she would hold for seven years, from 2004 to 2011. But controversy came knocking early on when on 10 April 2004, a 29-year-old police officer, Isaac Espinoza, was mindlessly shot down during his night shift for no apparent reason by 21-year-old David Hill, who was armed with an AK-47. Espinoza had been assigned duty in an area notorious for gang wars – Bayview-Hunters Point district – and was just about to end his shift when he and his partner noticed a young man moving around suspiciously. The officers pulled over to question the man, but he attacked Espinoza, shooting him point blank. Espinoza subsequently succumbed to his injuries. He was survived by his wife, Renata, and three-year-old daughter, Isabella.

The killing caused widespread outrage in the community. Espinoza's wife went into shock. The police fraternity was deeply disturbed by the incident and demanded the death penalty for the culprit, in accordance with the 'special circumstances' law that had been passed in California in 1973, which made the murderer of a police officer liable for the death penalty. Now, having taken the oath just a few months prior to the incident, the district attorney's new team was in the middle of a storm. While campaigning for the position of district attorney, Kamala had made it clear that she was against the death penalty, both personally and professionally, and she was not about to budge from her position. San Francisco juries had a reputation of shying away from the death penalty, which complicated matters. Added to that was the fact that the culprit was only 21 and not a hardened criminal, but in this case the district attorney's office was opposed to it. The Espinoza family and the entire police department were baffled by Kamala's stance. Especially since David Hill, the accused, had repeatedly been on the wrong side of the law since the age of ten. What fanned the controversy further was the fact that she made it clear from the beginning that her stand on the issue was unshakeable. Addressing the issue at a press conference, she said, 'In San Francisco, it is the will, I believe, of a majority of people that the most severe crimes be met with the most severe consequences. And that life without the possibility of parole is a severe consequence.' Although she was prompt in addressing the media and making her stance clear, Kamala neither investigated whether the accused could have been charged with a capital crime nor did she take the more compassionate position of waiting until after Espinoza's funeral. She was criticized for ignoring public sentiment before making her statement at the press conference.

Gary Delagnes, president of the San Francisco Police Officers Association, standing beside the district attorney during the press conference, was completely taken aback by her statement. Years later, in a CNN feature, he recalled, 'I'm standing there and I'm going, "Oh my God, the kid's not even in the ground yet." You're thinking to yourself, "Okay, is she sorry that this kid died or is this just a political opportunity? Is this just an opportunity for her to double down on the fact she's not going to pursue the death penalty?"'

Isaac Espinoza's funeral was attended by hundreds of police officers, and state and city officials. Senator Dianne Feinstein took the podium to deliver the eulogy. Without naming Kamala, who was also present at the funeral, she condemned the latter's adamant attitude. 'This is not only the definition of tragedy, it's the special circumstance called for by the death penalty law,' she said. Her words were met by resounding applause from everyone present. However, Kamala stuck to her guns. On 23 April, in an opinion piece that appeared in the *San Francisco Chronicle*, she wrote, 'For those who want this defendant put to death, let me say simply that there can be no exception to principle.' She added, 'I gave my word to the people of San Francisco that I oppose the death penalty and I will honor that commitment despite the strong emotions evoked by this case. I have heard and considered those pleas very carefully and I understand and share the pain that drives them, but my decision is made and it is final.' She added emphatically, 'The district attorney is charged with seeking justice, not vengeance.'

The matter became a topic of discussion in the country, especially in California. In Sacramento, 43 of the 80 members in the assembly, including several Democrats, signed a resolution urging that then attorney general of California Bill Lockyer and the United States Attorney's office in San Francisco look into the issue and arbitrate if required. Eventually, the resolution did not get to the floor for a vote. It died without a hearing in the Assembly Public Safety Committee. Since then, however, the police and Kamala have shared a cold and strained relationship.

Despite the setback, Kamala's track record as a district attorney was stellar. Before she took over, the felony conviction rate in the state had been 50 per cent but by 2009 it increased to 76 per cent, as reported by the *San Francisco Examiner*. Convictions of drug dealers also increased from 56 per cent in

2003 to 74 per cent in 2006 and the conviction rate for homicides rose to 85 per cent.

❧

Pragmatic, articulate and audacious, witty and spirited, Kamala had by now established a reputation for herself. She could take on anyone and she was not afraid to fight for the people. She could tackle any kind of pressure, but would not budge from her word or principles. While she had scored spectacular electoral victories, first as district attorney of San Francisco and then as attorney general of California, perhaps her biggest accomplishment was winning the settlement with the big banks during the housing crisis – an issue that plagued California and several other states. Kamala was able to negotiate an additional $12 billion in debt relief for Californians as part of the settlement of a 49-state suit against the country's five prominent banks (Bank of America, JPMorgan Chase, CitiFinancial GMAC/Ally Financial, and Wells Fargo), all indicted for mortgage abuses. It was a historic mortgage settlement that helped over 84,000 families in California. The landmark success of the win fetched Kamala much national attention. A *New York Times* report stated, 'In the end, she walked away with far more than California was slated to receive in the early days of the talks and a little more than was on the table as recently as January. Beaming into the cameras… she said California homeowners were guaranteed $12 billion in debt reduction, while most other states received only promises.'

Kamala had initially brokered a $25 billion settlement deal with the banks for illegally foreclosing on homeowners. She made it a point to not just do the paperwork but to also meet the victims of foreclosure, assuring them that their rights were being protected. Working tirelessly with members of the assembly and the Senate, she drafted the Homeowner Bill of Rights, which was meant to protect homeowners from practices that were detrimental to their interests, such as robo-signing and dual tracking. The bill also provided for the assignment of a single-point contact at financial institutions for homeowners to connect with to gain greater clarity on matters pertaining to their property. An article in SFGate.com commended her efforts, saying, 'Attorney General Harris announced a much-needed Homeowner Bill of Rights, a set of laws designed to stop deceptive practices by banks and help families keep their homes. This comes just weeks after Harris' shrewd negotiating tactics won California the lion's share of a $26 billion multistate settlement with big banks over foreclosure abuses.'

According to a 2013 report by the attorney general's California Monitor Program, California homeowners received $18.4 billion in mortgage relief. Kamala's decision to pull out of an earlier settlement deal for greater monetary benefit of those affected by the foreclosures did not find much support at first. However, in the end her decision paid off. 'Ultimately, she negotiated a deal that guarantees $12 billion in debt reduction for Californians whose homes are underwater and will provide about $2,000 each for families whose homes were taken – often without any legal due process,' reported SFGate.com.

Kamala has also been commended for her work on the prevention of human trafficking and her consistently tough stance on the war on drugs.

During her time as attorney general, she made it a priority to prosecute transnational gangs involved in trafficking drugs, firearms and humans. 'Human trafficking is a growing threat because criminal organizations have determined it is a low-risk, high-reward crime. We are here to change that calculus. We must counter the ruthlessness of human traffickers with resolve and collaboration. Law enforcement must continue to train, gather data, and shut down the trafficking operations in our state,' Kamala said in a press statement on Human Trafficking Trends in California and Law Enforcement Responses.

In 2014, the attorney general was honoured for rape kit processing, with her office's Rapid DNA Service Team being the proud recipient of the United States Department of Justice's Award for Professional Innovation in Victim Services. On this count, Associated Press reported, 'The state attorney general's office is receiving national recognition for accelerating the testing of rape kits, using innovations that have been adopted by eight of California's 58 counties.' The report revealed that the state-of-the-art programme automated DNA testing, tripling the number of cases that could be handled and reducing processing time to 15 days. With the help of the programme, a backlog of 1,300 rape cases in state-run laboratories was eliminated.

Kamala's work in environmental protection too has been widely acknowledged. At a time when many people in positions of power were busy refuting the very existence of climate change, her take on the issue was refreshing.

As district attorney of San Francisco, she created the office's first Environmental Justice Unit in 2005, and while serving as attorney general of California she furthered the cause by taking bold steps for environmental protection and drafting several laws to do this. Her view was that the environment suffered because there was no accountability and this would need to change by means of legal as well as criminal liabilities.

Through the years Kamala has been involved with either introducing or co-sponsoring environmental reforms and legislations, such as the Environmental Justice for All Act, Stop Arctic Ocean Drilling Act, Close Big Oil Tax Loopholes Act, Climate Equity

Act, COAST Anti-Drilling Act, Living Shorelines Act and Zero-Emissions Vehicles Act. She also worked on a resolution opposing former President of the United States Donald Trump's efforts to withdraw from the Paris Agreement in 2017. As a member of the Senate Committee on Environment and Public Works, Kamala issued a statement on 1 June 2017, expressing concern and displeasure at his decision. It read: 'We can all agree that all people should be able to breathe clean air and live in a safe and healthy environment. Pulling out of the Paris Agreement is an irrational decision that is a disastrous step backward, threatens the viability of our planet for future generations, and abdicates our role of leadership. The United States has an obligation to combat this global threat to public health and safety here at home, and abroad. As this Administration retreats, I will continue to work to support California's efforts to lead the fight against global climate change.'

On 7 November 2007, about 53,000 gallons of bunker fuel spilled into the bay when a container ship, the *Cosco Busan*, rammed into the San Francisco–Oakland Bay Bridge, threatening severe damage to the flora and fauna of the region. 'Workers attempted to save wildlife, but the death toll was large despite their efforts. An estimated 6,849 birds and between 14 and 29 per cent of spawning herring that winter were killed, according to government regulators,' stated a report in SFGate.com. The Department of Justice, along with the State of California, the City and County of San Francisco, and the City of Richmond signed and lodged a consent decree requiring Regal Stone Limited and Fleet Management Limited, the owners and operators of MV *Cosco Busan* to pay damages. In September 2011, Kamala secured a $44.4 million settlement for the clean-up and restoration of the San Francisco Bay. 'This Bay is the jewel of the San Francisco region and the *Cosco Busan* oil spill left a lasting scar across our water, natural habitats and wildlife,' Kamala said at a press conference. 'This settlement will allow all of these precious resources to be restored to their original health and beauty,' she added.

The years 2015 and 2016 too were quite eventful for Kamala on the environmental front. After the unfortunate Refugio oil spill in 2015, Kamala toured the coastline and ordered for possible criminal violations to be looked into. The oil spill in question had deposited about 140,000 gallons of crude oil off the coast of Santa Barbara, California. During this time she also secured numerous multi-million-dollar settlements from fuel service companies such as Chevron, British Petroleum, ARCO, Phillips 66, and ConocoPhillips. The companies were accused of failing to efficiently monitor hazardous materials in their underground storage tanks used to store fuel for retail sale at a large number of California's gas stations and thus causing severe environmental damage to surrounding areas. Another high-profile settlement was arranged by Kamala with the automobile giant Volkswagen, which had to pay up to $14.7 billion to federal and California regulators and the owners of the 475,000 polluting diesel vehicles. The claims were related to the company's use of defeat devices to exhibit permissible emissions standards on its diesel automobiles between 2009 and 2015, while the rigged vehicles were actually emitting as much as 40 times the allowed limit of harmful nitrogen oxides. According to a *San Francisco Chronicle* report, 'Under the settlement approved by US District Judge Charles Breyer of San Francisco, VW [Volkswagen] will pay $76 million to attorney general Kamala Harris' office for expenses in the legal case and the costs of enforcing consumer-protection and environmental laws.' It also added, 'The remaining $10 million will fund studies on the health impacts of auto emissions and the detection of cheating devices attached to emissions systems. Harris' office says it is the largest settlement the state has won from an automaker.'

Kamala is firmly of the view that society can only be free of crime if there is a resolve to focus on rehabilitation over reprimand; that juvenile and adult offenders involved in petty and non-violent crimes especially do not belong in prisons but can be guided towards becoming responsible citizens – and she has backed her beliefs with decisive action.

As district attorney of San Francisco, a reform programme she initiated in 2005 called 'Back on Track' received rave reviews. Under this programme, first-time non-violent offenders between the ages of 18 and 30, mostly first-time felons and low-level drug sellers, were given a chance to go back to civil life and contribute to society. According to the Bureau of Justice Assistance, those enrolled in the programme needed to attend an orientation session and take part in intensive community service for a six-week probationary period. Only those who completed six weeks of community service were eligible for enrolment. Once they pleaded guilty to the charges and their formal sentencing was deferred, they could begin a rigorous 12- to 18-month programme with goals set by an individualized Personal Responsibility Plan (PRP). The PRP mandated concrete achievements in employment, education, parenting and child support, and required participants to perform up to 220 hours of community service. In addition, participants in the programme were to be closely supervised and their progress evaluated. Those graduating from the programme were expected to find employment, enrol into school full-time, clear drug tests if required, and comply with all the terms of their PRPs. When they graduated, the court would dismiss the original case and give them a clean chit.

About the programme, Kamala wrote in a report in the *Huffington Post* in 2010, 'Police and prosecutors are deluged with low-level drug cases, and the public spends billions on prisons to house these offenders. And, every year, prisons release hundreds of thousands of these offenders back into our communities. They're sent back with a bus ticket and a little cash in hand – and that's about it. They have no plan, no skills, nowhere to go, and no other changed circumstances. They pick up right where they left off... Within three years of release, seven out of ten California prisoners will re-offend and return to prison.' She also said, 'After decades of this sad cycle, our prisons are swollen beyond capacity and our budgets maxed. Across the country, leaders are acknowledging that we've been missing a crucial opportunity all along. Perhaps the most crucial step in the criminal justice process is the most often ignored – what happens after the conviction and prison sentence, when the prisoner comes home.'

The Back on Track programme garnered much admiration for its effectiveness and has been acknowledged by the Department of Justice as a model for re-entry programmes across the country. It also saved taxpayers' money. The cost incurred for every participant in the programme was about $5,000, a stark contrast to the total expense of holding the prisoner in jail through their trial period – $10,000 to adjudicate a case and nearly $50,000 per year to house a low-level offender in prison. The programme was adopted in other counties in California, and later in Atlanta, Brooklyn, Dallas and many more cities.

Another matter that was a cause of grave concern for Kamala was truancy. While running for attorney general, Kamala had begun a speech at San Francisco's Commonwealth Club with the words, 'I believe that a child going without an education is tantamount to a crime.' Truancy was a big problem in many states in America, and particularly in California – and Kamala was well aware that the issue was not going to solve itself. In official reports drafted by her, Kamala mentioned that in San Francisco alone over 94 per cent of all homicide victims under the age of 25 were high school dropouts, while statewide, two-thirds of prison inmates were high school dropouts. Believing that some hard steps needed to be taken, Kamala launched a programme in 2006 that involved someone from the district attorney's office visiting parents and issuing them letters that warned them of the legal implications of their children's truancy. The fine imposed on parents whose children played truant was $2,500 and the parents could be jailed for up to a year. This was considered an extreme step by her detractors and Kamala was regarded as being unsympathetic as families with truant children were already troubled and also faced financial issues. On the other hand, supporters of the programme pointed to figures illustrating that school attendance rates in San Francisco rose after the implementation of the programme. Later, in 2011, when she continued her fight against truancy as the state's attorney general, Kamala stuck to her belief in criminal penalties for parents of truant children. She believed that preventing truancy had significant positive consequences. Children engaged productively in schools were less likely to fall prey to the lure of criminal gangs or be drawn into a life of crime.

For years, the controversies surrounding Kamala's anti-truancy measures refused to die down, even as she expressed regret at the stringent manner in which the scheme was executed. She also conveyed her sorrow at the treatment of some of the parents who were, in fact, jailed. 'My regret is that I have now heard stories where, in some jurisdictions, district attorneys have criminalized the parents. And I regret that that has happened,' she told the *Los*

Angeles Times in April 2019. 'And the thought that anything that I did could have led to that, because that certainly was not the intention – never was the intention.'

Observers have pointed out that Kamala's approach to handling crime is rather unconventional. Instead of following age-old laws and practices, she has been working to upgrade the system for practical outcomes. She looks beyond one-size-fits-all punishments, with a sharp focus on reform and life after prison. She explains her perspective brilliantly in her book *Smart on Crime: A Career Prosecutor's Plan to Make Us Safer*: 'The problem is that we have been using only the tools best suited to combatting the offenders at the top of the pyramid, and we have been using them on the entire crime pyramid. Most nonviolent offenders are learning the wrong lesson, and in many cases, they are becoming better and more hardened criminals during their prison stays. It's time to rock the crime pyramid.' She points out that these offenders, more often than not, are victims of drug abuse and are rarely skilled in any trade. When they are housed in jails they are pushed further into the grip of criminal gangs in jail, and after their prison stay all they are left with is a bus ticket home and some money. Kamala illustrates in her book that this way of dealing with crime forces them into a life of more crime. Instead, she has always laid greater emphasis on prison alternatives, reform programmes like Back on Track and shorter sentences for non-violent crimes.

5

A TASTE FOR POLITICS

'What I want young women and girls to know is: You are powerful and your voice matters… You're going to walk into many rooms in your life and career where you may be the only one who looks like you or who has had the experiences you've had. But you remember that when you are in those rooms, you are not alone. We are all in that room with you applauding you on. Cheering your voice. And just so proud of you. So you use that voice and be strong.'

– **Kamala Harris**, in an interview with *Marie Claire*

IN 1994 KAMALA'S PERSONAL AND PROFESSIONAL LIFE
switched to a higher gear.

At the time the deputy district attorney of
Alameda County, Kamala had fallen in love with one
of the nation's most brilliant politicians, California
state assembly speaker Willie Brown. He was thirty
years her senior, but that was not all – he was also
married. Despite the years between them, they
had much in common. They had both risen from
scratch, though Brown's path had been particularly
tough, coming as he did from Texas during the days
of Jim Crow, a series of local and state laws that
enforced racial segregation in southern United States
from 1877 till the beginning of the Civil Rights
Movement in the 1950s. While Brown was still
married at the time he was dating Kamala, he had

been estranged from his wife since 1981. He lived his life like an open book, making no bones about dating other women. Eventually, when it became clear to Kamala that Brown would never officially call it quits with his wife, she split up with him in 1995, after roughly two years of being in limbo.

Kamala made it a point not to talk about their complicated relationship or discuss Brown in public. In a rare statement about him to SFWeekly.com in 2003, while she was running for the post of San Francisco's district attorney, she referred to him as an 'albatross hanging around my neck'. The report stated, 'The mere mention of their former liaison makes her shoulders tense, her hands clench, and her eyes narrow. "I refuse," she says vehemently, "to design my campaign around criticizing Willie Brown for the sake of appearing to be independent when I have no doubt that I am independent of him – and that he would probably right now express some fright about the fact that he cannot control me. His career is over; I will be alive and kicking for the next 40 years. I do not owe him a thing."' Brown on the other hand never refrained from making stray comments about Kamala throughout the time they were together and in the years following that. In

2019, when he was well into his 80s, he said on a radio show that he had not been as dedicated to the relationship as she had been. He also acknowledged the imbalance in their relationship through his telling statement, 'It was a real love affair. I loved me and she loved me.'

It was also common knowledge that Brown used his power to open some doors for Kamala early in her career. However, once those doors were flung open, Kamala paved her own path, proving herself every step of the way. In 1994 Brown appointed her on the Unemployment Insurance Appeals Board, the state board accountable for hearing appeals from people who were not provided with unemployment benefits, and Kamala left her job as Alameda County deputy district attorney for the new position. In late November 1994, Brown transferred her to another part-time board that oversaw California's medical contracts – the California Medical Assistance Commission. The move did not go unnoticed by the media. A *Los Angeles Times* report in November 1994 said, 'Brown, exercising his power even as his speakership seems near an end, named Attorney Kamala Harris to the California Medical Assistance Commission, a job that pays $72,000 a year,' while also speculating on the exact nature of their relationship. She continued to hold the same post through 1998, three years after their relationship was over.

Brown, who went on to become the mayor of San Francisco and was the first African American to hold the office, never shied away from speaking publicly about his influence on the politics of California. In a brief statement to *SFGate* he stated, 'Sure, I dated Kamala Harris. So what?' He mentioned that he had certainly helped her career, but that he 'also helped the careers of House Speaker Nancy Pelosi, Governor Gavin Newsom, Senator Dianne Feinstein and a host of other politicians. The difference is that Harris is the only one who, after I helped her, sent word that I would be indicted if I "so much as jaywalked" while she was D.A. [of San Francisco].'

In September 2004, during her first year as San Francisco's district attorney, Kamala, who was always scanning the political scene, co-hosted a fundraiser at the Four Seasons Hotel. It was for a fellow traveller, a senator from Illinois, Chicago, who worked for a humble law firm and lectured on constitutional law at the University of Chicago on the side. His name was Barack Obama. Their meeting marked the beginning of a friendship that would last for years. In fact, Kamala would often be referred to as 'an early Obama backer' and 'the female Obama', especially after his ascent to the position of President of the United States in 2009.

Though there were several black politicians on the scene, Kamala and Obama were often compared to each other – for obvious reasons. They were both part black, part not; both had a background in law and both reflected the changing face of the Democratic Party. *Ebony* magazine, in its May 2006 edition, named the two among the 100 most influential black Americans – the future President ranked at number 67, and Kamala Harris at number 5.

As the years progressed, their friendship and professional admiration for each other continued to grow. In February 2007, Kamala travelled to the cruelly cold Springfield in Illinois, Chicago, for the launch of Obama's presidential campaign. Within a month of the commencement of the campaign she had become the most vocal and prominent elected official in California to endorse Obama. Her support was unwavering through to the end of the campaign. On the night of 4 November 2008, she joined thousands of deliriously happy people who gathered at Chicago's Grant Park to celebrate her friend's historic win.

In 2013, when Kamala was serving as the attorney general of California, while addressing a fundraiser for the Democratic National Committee in San Francisco, Obama had referred to her as the 'best-looking attorney general in the country'. The remark sparked reactions from people who deemed it as being sexist. Obama's words had been, 'You have to be careful to, first of all, say she is brilliant and she is dedicated and she is tough, and she is exactly what you'd want in anybody who is administering the law, and making sure that everybody is getting a fair shake... She also happens to be, by far, the best-looking attorney general in the country.' When the people in the crowd started laughing, he added, 'It's true! C'mon.' While some argued that he had undermined her body of work with this comment, others said that it had been misconstrued and blown out of proportion. White House spokesperson Jay Carney, in a briefing, said about the incident, 'They are old friends and good friends, and he did not want in any way to diminish the attorney general's

professional accomplishments and her capabilities.'
The political world and the media were divided on
the issue. Articles with headlines such as 'Obama
in Need of Gender-Sensitivity Training' made the
rounds. After the controversy, Obama promptly
called Kamala to apologize if he had caused her any
offence and they continued to be on excellent terms.

In fact, Obama lent unwavering support to
the Biden–Harris campaign. He also interviewed
her for Joe Biden's YouTube channel in September
2020 – quizzing her about Biden and the secret of
staying upbeat through the campaign trail. He asked
her, 'Even with the support of the family it can still
be gruelling. Any trade secret?' To which Kamala
replied, 'I work out every morning regardless of
how much sleep I have had. It's just the best way to
start the day. During the pandemic I couldn't order
weights…they were all sold out…so I used water
bottles.' She also added, with her signature laughter,
that she gets her groove on with her workout
playlist. 'I've got my playlist, you know. I love some
Mary J. Blige.'

Joe Biden and Kamala Harris had also been
acquainted professionally for a long time. Since
announcing her Senate candidacy in January 2015,

Kamala had been busy securing endorsements and raising funds. She used as a launching pad the tightly knit world of San Francisco high society. Having ably cultivated relationships with influential people who would become friends as well as donors to her political campaigns, Kamala fell back on these reliable resources when she needed them. The list of those who backed her included Hollywood stars such as Rob Reiner, Barbara Streisand, Sean Penn, Mark and Susie Buell, and Silicon Valley venture capitalists. As a result of her connections, she began to be seen as someone with an objective political ambition and with political utility.

Determined to win the endorsement of the California Democratic Party, in February 2016, she made a call to then vice president Joe Biden and asked if he would come to the state party convention in San Jose. By this time, Donald Trump had taken over the White House and things were beginning to look grim. Biden obliged, and showed support by singling out Kamala, recalling that she shared a great bond with his beloved son Beau, who had succumbed to brain cancer the year before. Nearly 45 minutes into the one-hour-long speech, Biden reiterated a theme that was close to his heart –

one he would make during his 2020 presidential campaign as well: 'Our people are not the problem. Our politics is the problem. It has grown so petty, so personal, so angry, so ugly.' His bid was to clean up the political scene along with representatives of the people, like Kamala. With Biden's blessings, the California Democratic Party too endorsed Kamala. Added to this was President Obama's endorsement, which Kamala already had in her kitty.

Kamala and Trump's association, if not very strong or positive, goes all the way back to 2011, five years before he would take over from her friend Obama as the President of the country. It is a common practice for politicians to make their way to New York in pursuit of campaign money, just as politicians from New York and other states travel to California for the same thing. In September 2011, Kamala too set her sights on Manhattan with a desire to raise money and build a national profile. Eric Schneiderman, who was serving as New York's attorney general at the time, helped her pull in a crowd with the help of another New York lawyer who represented an impressive clientele before state attorneys general. Donald J. Trump was among the New Yorkers who donated to Kamala's campaign on that trip through a $5,000 check dated 26 September 2011, followed by another $1,000 on 20 February 2013. The next year, Trump's daughter Ivanka added another $2,000 to the tally on 3 June 2014. According to a report in USAToday. com, 'Harris' campaign spokesman Ian Sams told McClatchy that Harris donated the $6,000 Trump had contributed to a nonprofit that advocates for civil and human rights for Central Americans. But that donation wasn't made until 2015, a year after she won her reelection for attorney general and as she was launching her run for the Senate.' With businesses in several states, including California, it made perfect sense for the Trumps to keep themselves in the good books of the state's attorney. Their equation, however, was all set to change in the coming years.

6

GAME, SET, MATCH

'As a single, professional woman in my forties, and very much in the public eye, dating wasn't easy. I knew that if I brought a man with me to an event, people would immediately start to speculate about our relationship. I also knew that single women in politics are viewed differently than single men. We don't get the same latitude when it comes to our social lives.'

– **Kamala Harris**, *The Truths We Hold:*
An American Journey

KAMALA, WHO HAD ALWAYS BEEN INTENSELY PROTECTIVE about her private life, found dating to be rather challenging and complicated. Her position of power possibly intimidated most men. And who could blame them. The woman was wielding the law enforcement of the entire state of California, no less. And so, when she finally started dating entertainment litigator Douglas Emhoff in 2013, she kept it much under wraps so that the two could have a real shot at it, away from the prying eyes of the media.

Doug, who had a Juris Doctor degree from the University of Southern California Gould School of Law, had built quite a reputation in Los Angeles, with several A-listers from Hollywood on his client list. Chrisette Hudlin, who was an old friend of Kamala, and her husband, film-maker Reginald

Hudlin, were consulting with Doug to resolve a complicated legal issue. Before they parted, Chrisette asked Doug if he was single. In her memoir Kamala recounts how the conversation went.

Doug was curious. 'Why are you asking?'

She explained to him that she wanted to set him up with a single friend of hers, whom she had known for thirty years. His next question was obviously for her name.

'Kamala Harris,' Chrisette replied.

Having worked with scores of actors, directors, producers and musicians, he thought the name was familiar but couldn't exactly figure out who it was. Chrisette told him that it was the California attorney general she was talking about.

'Oh my god, she is hot,' Doug exclaimed.

She finally gave Kamala's number to Doug, cautioning him that it was not to be disclosed. She also told him not to mess it up, or else the Hudlins would take their legal business to another law firm. Chrisette then called Kamala to tell her about Doug and that she should be getting a call from him soon. 'He's cute and he's the managing partner of his law firm and I think you're really going to like him,' she said.

Doug sent her a text the same night while he was at a Lakers game. She replied to his text. In the morning, Doug fought an urge to call her, which he eventually gave in to. Kamala didn't answer the call and it went straight to voice mail. According to Doug, it was a really lame voice mail message (that he contemplated explaining with another message), but at least it made her call him back. Kamala now plays the voice mail every year on their anniversary. She told him she was visiting Los Angeles that weekend and they decided to meet. Doug told Chasten Buttigieg, husband of former South Bend mayor Pete Buttigieg, in a YouTube interview for his show Chasten Chats With, recalling how they were set up. 'I was just a dude as a lawyer, and then I met Kamala on a blind date set up by legendary film-maker Reginald Hudlin.'

Doug was not intimidated by Kamala, probably because they were both lawyers, though their areas of work were completely different. While she was in the public eye, he specialized in entertainment and intellectual property law. 'When I met her it just felt like another busy successful lawyer, who happened to live in San Francisco. She was fighting the banks at that time for a settlement,' he told Buttigieg.

Kamala mentions in her memoir that the morning after their first date Doug wasted no time in arranging the second one. 'I'm too old to play games or hide the ball. I really like you, and I want to see if we can make this work,' he said in an email which, incidentally, also included his schedule for the next couple of months so that it would be easier for them to plan dates. The fact that he didn't beat around the bush and was open about expressing his feelings earned him brownie points. Getting down to the logistical details by emailing his schedule also showed that he was ready to invest in the relationship. 'We were falling in love and building a relationship. I was a single dad, so on the weekends that I wouldn't have the kids, I'd fly to San Francisco,' he told Buttigieg. 'As luck would have it, the law firm I was at asked me to open a San Francisco office. It was great. I would spend the whole week up there.'

Their relationship thrived under the radar. They did not even let some of their closest friends into their secret until things got serious.

After their second date, Doug was keen on introducing her to his teenage kids. While Kamala was interested in meeting them as well, she did feel

86

it was too soon. 'As a child of divorce, I knew how hard it can be when your parents start to date other people. And I was determined not to insert myself in their lives until Doug and I had established we were in this for the long haul. Children need consistency; I didn't want to insert myself into their lives as a temporary fixture because I didn't want to disappoint them. There's nothing worse than disappointing a child,' she wrote in an essay for *Elle* magazine. 'So I slowed things down.'

Things started moving in a more serious direction after their third date and the two of them made some decisions about the course of their relationship. 'We agreed to commit to each other for six months, and to reevaluate our relationship at the end of it,' Kamala writes in her memoir. There it was. A matter-of-fact decision made by two adults, one who had never been married, and the other who had been for a long time and had two kids. Doug Emhoff, of Jewish descent, was married for 16 years before he and his wife Kerstin went their separate ways. Kerstin is the founder and CEO of the successful production company Prettybird, based in Los Angeles, and has also personally won a News and Documentary Emmy. They have two children together, Cole and Ella, who are named after the jazz legends, John Coltrane and Ella Fitzgerald.

In those six months, Kamala finally met the kids, holding a tin of chocolate chip cookies to which she had tied a bow in a red ribbon. 'When the day finally came, I had butterflies in my stomach. The plan was to go to a seafood hut off the Pacific Coast Highway called the Reel Inn, a favourite of the kids,' she revealed in her essay for *Elle*. The kids were a crucial factor in sealing the deal. 'Cole and Ella could not have been more welcoming. They are brilliant, talented, funny kids who have grown to be remarkable adults. I was already hooked on Doug, but I believe it was Cole and Ella who reeled me in,' she wrote. Once they crossed the six-month mark with the spark still intact, she brought Doug into her professional world by inviting him to a speech she was giving about truancy.

They continued to date for about a year after that before Doug proposed to her in her apartment. 'In March 2014, Emhoff had planned to propose while they were on vacation in Florence, but he popped the question while she was hurriedly packing and they were discussing what kind of takeout to order.

When she realized Emhoff's "I want to spend my life with you" wasn't just a sweet comment but a prelude to a marriage proposal, Harris burst into tears,' reveals an article in the *Washington Post*. The rest is history.

Kamala and Doug, both 49, tied the knot five months later, on 22 August 2014, in an intimate ceremony at the Santa Barbara County courthouse. The beautiful mission-style building is a much-favoured and coveted wedding location in southern California. Maya Harris officiated over the nuptials and even helped write the vows. Kamala mentions in her memoir that she followed the Indian tradition of placing a garland around her groom's neck, while Doug stomped on a glass, as is tradition in Jewish weddings. The bride did not forget about her family in India, as her uncle and aunt flew in to be a part of her special day. One of her maternal aunts, who is settled in Canada, also flew down. 'The wedding was a family affair with our family, his family and very close friends attending it. There was a Jewish ceremony as well as an Indian ceremony with mangalsutra, etc.,' Kamala's aunt Dr Sarala Gopalan, told Rediff.com. 'There was vegetarian food for us at the feast as she knew we eat only vegetarian food. Though she missed her mother, both of us chittis were there. The labels on the table were Sarala Chitti, Subhash Chittappa, etc.,' she added.

Once the wedding rituals were over, the couple threw a party for their friends at the Presidio Officers' Club in San Francisco. 'She looked truly very happy,' said Erin Lehane, a friend, who works for the State Building and Construction Trades Council of California. In each other, Kamala and Doug had found their running mates for life.

Doug's teenage children are very fond of their stepmother. However, the children never thought the title fit Kamala and decided to address her as 'Momala', a term of endearment that has found a place on one of her Twitter handles. After being named the Democratic nominee for vice president, Kamala said, 'I've had a lot of titles over my career, and certainly "vice president" will be great. But "Momala" will always be the one that means the most.' Doug also told Buttigieg during the interview that they are one big happy family, revealing that his first wife Kerstin is still a part of his life and is on good terms with Kamala. As Kamala mentions in the *Elle* essay, the four of them – Cole, Ella, Doug and her – get together to share family time over Sunday dinner. 'We come together, all of us around the table, and over time we've fallen into our roles. Cole sets the table and picks the music, Ella makes beautiful desserts, Doug acts as my sous-chef, and I cook.'

Since the year of their marriage, people have been witnessing Doug participating actively in the Harris campaign trail. He was a regular presence during the 2016 and 2019 campaigns as well – from fending off brash protesters to offering his wife a shoulder to lean on during exhausting days – his support was unwavering. Kamala recently said in an interview with Now This News, 'I love my husband. He is funny. He is kind. He is patient. He loves my cooking. He's just a really great guy.' It was Doug who held the Bible at Kamala's swearing-in ceremony as a senator in January 2017. When Kamala ended her presidential run in 2019, he shared her disappointment. 'She made that decision, and I would have supported whatever she decided,' he told *Marie Claire* in an interview. 'But I'm not her political adviser. I'm her husband. And so my role was to be there for her, to love her, to have her back, to talk it through, to help her.'

Doug took a leave of absence from his law firm, DLA Piper, where he worked as a litigator and partner, in August 2020 to support his wife in the vice presidential campaign. He didn't lobby for her while he was working there since the firm's Washington lobby arm represents defence contractors, health insurers, entertainment conglomerates and others.

After the swearing-in ceremony, Doug will officially don the title of the 'first second gentleman'. He has already shown immense support for his wife, being actively by her side throughout the campaign trail. As Kamala prepares to take on a position in the White House held only by men so far, Doug, too, is gearing up for a role previously played by women. For starters, in November 2020, as the couple prepared to move into the White House, Doug quit his job. 'Doug is not the first male political spouse, and yet it is – still – thrilling to see a man put a pause on his own ambitions for those of his wife,' said an article in the *Guardian,* titled 'More Than a Second Gentleman: Why Doug Emhoff is Kamala Harris' Secret Weapon', by Hadley Freeman. 'A political leader's relationship with their partner reflects and also sets a national mood, from the Kennedys' broken illusion of perfection in 60s America, to the

Blairs' bolshie self-confidence in late 90s Britain. With Harris's marriage, we see a softening of gender roles, and a couple who married, not for children or social expectations, but because they just really dig each other.' He has already earned himself a fan base on social media called the #DougHive.

As Doug put it wittily in an interview to *Marie Claire*, 'I'm not overly political. I'm overly her husband.'

7

COURAGE, NOT COURTESY

'There will be people who say to you, "You are out of your lane." They are burdened by only having the capacity to see what has always been, instead of what can be. But don't you let that burden you.'

— **Kamala Harris**, at the Black Girls Lead conference, 2020

BAGGING THE TITLE OF THE FIRST INDIAN AMERICAN
senator was not an easy feat for Kamala. In the
election for the United States Senate in 2016, there
were key opponents challenging her claim. These
included big names such as the former Los Angeles
mayor Antonio Villaraigosa and lieutenant governor
Gavin Newsom. Then there was a formidable
opponent in Loretta Sanchez, who would not give
up without a fight. In the end, however, it was a clean
sweep. As the same news report concluded, 'From
the outset, the Senate race between Democrats
Harris and Orange County Rep. Loretta Sanchez
possessed an air of history in the making. California
had never before elected a black or Latino politician
to the United States Senate, and Harris will become

only the second black woman in the nation's history to serve in Congress' upper chamber.'

When, on 3 January 2017, Vice President Joe Biden administered the oath for the office of California's forty-fifth senator to Kamala Devi Harris, the daughter of immigrants who had come from India and Jamaica respectively in search of higher education and better lives, she became only the second black woman – and the first woman of Indian descent – to serve in this most elite position. She had already been advised by the best political minds in Washington and California on how to succeed in the Senate. The advice that resonated with her above all was to hire good staff and be ready for anything. She did that and more. But nothing could have prepared her, or the rest of the Senate, for the turmoil that commenced with the beginning of the session of Congress that followed.

Defying all expectations, the flamboyant tycoon Donald J. Trump had been elected President of the United States in November 2016, beating his rival Hillary Clinton by winning 304 electoral votes to Clinton's 227 and sweeping the states, though Clinton had won the popular vote by 2.8 million votes. From the time he assumed office, Trump seemed to be intent on undoing as many milestones as possible that had been achieved by Obama and Congressional Democrats during Obama's tenure. Trump's nominees for positions overseeing the process would undergo confirmation hearings to secure their positions immediately, in a Senate that was more bitterly divided along party lines than ever before. The environment was not conducive to initiate or execute any constructive policy at the time. The Republicans, who now controlled the Senate and the House of Representatives, nitpicked incessantly, bringing to a halt the progress made by the previous administration on critical issues such as immigration, the environment, health insurance, taxes and Supreme Court nominees. The Democrats were left helpless, capable of doing nothing more than protest.

To make matters worse, outgoing Obama administration officials shared serious concerns about an intelligence leak, implying that Trump's campaign team, and perhaps the President-elect himself, may have conspired with Russia to help him defeat Hillary Clinton. Now, they had to act quickly to document and safeguard incriminating information before Trump officially took over the White House on 20 January 2017.

Already in considerable distress, and with their hands mostly tied, the Democrats identified Kamala Harris, with 26 years of experience in law enforcement under her belt, as someone whose skills could be valuable when it came to grilling top officials of the Donald Trump administration like John Kelly, Jeff Sessions and Rod Rosenstein on the matter at hand. Not only did she possess immense courtroom experience and know the law like the back of her hand, but she had also emerged as someone who was not afraid to ask tough questions.

Kamala had meanwhile also been included by Senate Democratic Leader Chuck Schumer on many significant Senate committees, including one that is usually unlikely for newly appointed senators to be on: the Senate Intelligence Committee, or the Senate Intel Committee. Juggling her involvement in committees on intelligence, the Department of Homeland Security, environment and budget, Kamala thus became a front-line responder, trying to hold the Democratic line against several, if not all, of the issues at the core of Trump's agenda.

Senator Kamala Devi Harris's sixth day in office, 10 January 2017, heralded in troubled times. That morning, the Homeland Security Committee held a confirmation hearing for retired Marine Corps General John F. Kelly. A native of Boston, Kelly had stepped down in 2016 from the post of head of the United States Southern Command, in which capacity he had supervised all American military operations in Latin America and the Caribbean. Trump had nominated him for the powerful post of the Secretary of Homeland Security. If he got the position, which he was ultimately confirmed for on 20 January 2017, Kelly would be responsible for many issues of critical importance to the border state of California and the entire nation.

As the hearing proceeded, amidst the outpourings of support for the general, Kamala's line of questioning stood out as matter-of-fact and tough. Having thanked him cordially for his services and sacrifices for the country over the years, she proceeded to ask him if he intended to carry out Trump's stated plans to construct a border wall, deport thousands of people, expand the administration's enforcement authority and increase the number of detention cells nationwide. Such matters were of prime concern and interest in California where 31 per cent of the population is Latino and 27 per cent of the population is foreign born.

A major concern for Kamala was the Deferred Action for Childhood Arrivals (DACA) programme, and she got to it without delay. One of Obama's signature programmes, the DACA gave protection to scores of young people, popularly known as Dreamers, whose parents had crossed the border into the United States with their children, seeking employment opportunities and a better life for their families. Although Dreamers were not citizens of the United States, a great number of them had no real connection to their parents' home country. California has the highest number of Dreamers among all states – 183,000 to be exact. While most of them were studying in college, others were working. One of Trump's first announcements as President had been the initiative to deport them. Kamala rightly wanted to know where Kelly stood on the matter.

Kelly, however, did not commit to defending the DACA. Even after twenty Democratic members of the Congressional Hispanic Caucus pressed Kelly to take a stand and assure them that he would help preserve the programme, he refused to give them the answer they were looking for. He informed the lawmakers that he could not guarantee that the administration he served would defend it in court. He also said that he had consulted attorneys who had told him the programme would not survive a legal challenge. He went on to urge Congress to find a legislative solution, repeating several times, 'Congress should do something about it.'

In her questioning of Kelly, Kamala was courteous but straightforward. Her aim was to get answers to her questions, which she did. Kelly was suggesting, without asserting directly, that he would oversee a policy that would lead to the deportation of Dreamers. It would have been a massive blow for more than 150,000 people in Kamala's home state. Nine days later, Kamala issued a statement saying she would vote against Kelly, making her one of eleven senators to not extend Kelly their support. 'Unfortunately, I can't look Dreamers in the face and offer them any guarantee that General John Kelly won't deport them,' she said. 'And, without that guarantee, I can't support his nomination for the Department of Homeland Security. For ethical and moral reasons, we have to honour the promise made by the United States government to these kids.'

By the time the nation was barely a few months into the new government, Kamala had emerged as one of the Trump administration's most aggressive and eminent critics. She was quickly becoming a leader in the Democratic resistance to the Trump administration in the Senate and voiced her pledge in the election-night speech in 2016. 'Do not despair. Do not be overwhelmed,' she said. '[We cannot] throw up our hands when it is time to roll up our sleeves and fight for who we are.' Within and outside the Senate, she was beginning to be viewed as a representative of a new political generation in Washington.

Five months later, in June 2017 when the Senate Intelligence Committee was called to enquire into Trump's decision a month earlier to fire the director of the FBI, James Comey, Kamala was present as a member of the committee.

During the high-profile hearing, Kamala, a well-trained prosecutor, pointedly asked Deputy Attorney General Rod Rosenstein whether he would sign a letter to give Special Counsel Robert Mueller full independence from the Department of Justice in his probe, which would have the same effect as a letter issued to then Special Counsel Patrick

Fitzgerald for the investigation into the 2003 leak of covert Central Intelligence Agency (CIA) officer Valerie Plame's identity. As she doggedly questioned him, seeking only 'yes' or 'no' for an answer, the chairman of the committee Richard Burr cut her off and reprimanded her for not being 'courteous' enough. The move rankled many, who expressed their reactions to it on Twitter and pointed out that when women do their job well they get called 'hysterical'.

When Kamala made an attempt to explain her line of questioning, Burr cut her off yet again. The other Democrats on the committee stayed silent, but what Burr had not counted on was the televised hearing going viral almost immediately. To viewers and observers the exchange had come across as old White male senators 'shushing' Kamala Harris, the only black woman on the committee. As it exploded on Twitter and eventually other social media platforms, the spiteful bickering worsened among Democrat and Republican senators, and also between the Democrats and the Trump administration.

Hours later, Kamala and her staff, channelizing their indignation and capitalizing on the attention the episode had harboured, came up with a meme:

'Courage, Not Courtesy.' The meme went viral at a whole different level. In no time it appeared on merchandise, like stickers, mugs and T-shirts. 'RT this if you've ordered your "Courage, Not Courtesy" sticker and want your friends and family to get one too,' Kamala tweeted.

An article titled 'Kamala Harris Silencing Gives Rise to New Feminist Slogan', published in the *Huffington Post*, stated, 'Senator Harris announced her new slogan on Facebook. She follows the lead of other female politicians who turned berating reprimands into empowering slogans. While critics may see these moves as a political attempt to capitalize on a catch phrase, these slogans have a far deeper impact on social change.' The article also noted the trend of women in politics, such as Hillary Clinton and Senator Elizabeth Warren, using hurtful words by male politicians to their advantage, indicating that they will speak up, no matter what. When Clinton was referred to as a 'nasty woman' by Donald Trump during a 2016 presidential debate, she spun it around into an unapologetic slogan, and 'Nasty Girl' became a viral slogan in her campaign, signifying a powerful woman who will say what's on her mind. Similarly, in 2017, Senator Elizabeth Warren was shushed by Senate majority leader Mitch McConnell, as she was raising issue with the nomination of Jeff Sessions on the Senate floor. 'She was warned. She was given an explanation. Nevertheless, she persisted,' McConnell rebuked. Little did he know that 'Nevertheless, she persisted' would become a war cry for women across America.

'These slogans help women take back power over the very scenarios that seek to disenfranchise them. When women are reminded their place in society through reprimands and dis-empowering statements, the very re-appropriation of these statements helps women reshape the narrative,' concluded the article.

Six days later, Kamala would bring about her most viral moment.

On 13 June 2017, the Senate Intel Committee's witness was Jeff Sessions. As a senator from Alabama, Sessions had been the first major Republican to endorse Trump's presidential run in February 2016. He had been nominated by Trump to serve as the United States attorney general. Since taking office, Sessions had been under the radar for the possible collusion between the Trump administration and

Russian officials during the 2016 election. In March of 2017 it had been revealed that Sessions had failed to disclose that he had twice met with the Russian ambassador during his confirmation hearings. However, as attorney general, he followed the rules of the Justice Department and recused himself from the Trump–Russia probe, citing a conflict of interest stemming from his appointed role as the head of the Trump campaign's national security advisory council. This did not go down well with Trump, as it put a civil servant, Rosenstein, in charge of the investigation. The unfolding events put Sessions' testimony in the category of must-see television and the nation tuned in to watch Kamala's cross-examination of him. People were curious to know what she could draw out of him about possible links between Trump and Russia during and after his presidential campaign. They were also looking forward to finding out why Trump fired Comey, and about Trump's efforts to overturn the probe.

During this hearing, too, Kamala was part of the Senate Intel Committee. Her persistent questioning of the Trump administration officials had made her a rising star on the country's political stage. But, for the second time in a week, Senator Kamala

Harris was cut off by her Republican colleagues while posing her questions. When she asked Attorney General Jeff Sessions about his refusal to answer questions concerning conversations he may have had with President Donald Trump, she was interrupted by Arizona senator John McCain. Then, in almost an exact repeat of the proceedings of the previous week, Chairman Richard Burr stepped in, saying, 'Senators, we'll allow the chair to control the hearing. Senator Harris, let him answer the question.' Not backing down, Kamala persisted, rapidly firing questions at Sessions, visibly flustering him.

'I don't recall,' was Sessions's response to most questions he was asked.

She asked him whether he had made any acquaintance with Russian business leaders or intelligence operatives at the 2016 Republican National Convention in Cleveland, which, as it turned out, was a focus of Kremlin operations. He denied he had. Then he said he wanted to clarify his response since he had met many people in Cleveland. Kamala went on to press him, and an evidently flustered Sessions requested her to slow down with the questions.

But Kamala continued, undeterred, demanding more precise information from Sessions about what law or policy he was referring to when he said he couldn't discuss key issues or share documents with the committee.

Sessions replied, 'I'm not able to answer the question.' But that was not enough for Kamala.

She continued with her questions, though she was shushed frequently.

Later, Republican senators and conservative commentators blamed Kamala for being disrespectful, saying she had failed to follow Senate rules of order. It was evident that old-time Washington hands, particularly men who were not used to having strong women politicians around, were having trouble dealing with her audacity and doggedness, but to those who knew her back in California, there was no doubt that this was absolutely her way.

After the June 2017 hearings Kamala became one of the most talked-about politicians in the country. Not only were Republicans critical of her style, but some of her fellow Democrats and Homeland Security officials too were getting miffed at her. They did not have any political axe to grind, but still felt offended by her. A section of the Democrats assumed that her pugilistic tone was for theatrical effect, while others thought her desire for the spotlight was part of a long-term plan to 'pull an Obama' by staying in the Senate just long enough to get the credentials compulsory to run for President.

The issue that largely led to these assumptions and more was that Kamala had declined to meet many of the individuals nominated by Trump for the highest positions in Homeland Security. She decided to grill them in public confirmation hearings, demanding yes-or-no answers to tricky questions that could not be answered in simple ways. This rubbed some officials the wrong way. The Trump nominees' failure or refusal to answer her questions certainly made for good sound bites. But it did little to deliver answers to the community at large about some of the most significant policy issues of the day and didn't help to promote the kind of good governance required for the Senate to succeed at its role as an overseer. Perhaps, most notably, it didn't help nurture productive relationships between top department officials and the senator who oversaw them. Conventionally, the issues she brought up in public hearings would have first been discussed in private meetings. Known as courtesy calls, such meetings are held at the end of a thorough course conducted for the select few political appointees considered to be so critical to the department's mission that they require confirmation by the full Senate.

In spring 2017, Elaine Duke, nominated by President Trump to the second highest ranking position in the Department of Homeland Security, sought a meeting with all the members of the Homeland Security Committee. She particularly wanted to meet the Democrats in order to offer them in-depth answers to issues that were in the headlines. She wanted to address matters that seemed too complex for the structure of a public hearing. A career civil servant, Duke, who is largely seen as an apolitical moderate, had spent almost three decades in public service, working in the administrations of George W. Bush and Barack Obama before Trump's. Almost all the Senate's Democrats obliged her with a private meeting, but not Kamala. She asked her questions in public.

Under normal circumstances, Kamala's brash confidence and unapologetic ambition would have created more friction within the ultra-competitive Senate. But the timing of her arrival proved to be a stroke of good luck. From the beginning of the eventful 115th Congress, the Senate's Democrats quickly grasped that they faced a far greater threat from the Trump administration than they did from each other. Most of the Democrat senators realized they needed to join hands to work together and that there was no use taking shots at each other. Many of the staffers who make the Senate function found Kamala to be a lot more approachable than most of her colleagues, making her one of the go-to senators around. That, in turn, paid off handsomely for her.

She had arrived.

8

THE CHOSEN ONE

'Anyone who claims to be a leader must speak like a leader. That means speaking with integrity and truth.'

– **Kamala Harris**, Instagram post, 2019

ON 28 AND 29 JULY 2018, KAMALA GATHERED EVERYONE
of relevance in her personal and professional life at
Maya Harris's Manhattan apartment next to Central
Park, to review the most significant decision of
her career.

Her consultants – Ace Smith, Sean Clegg,
Juan Rodriguez and Dan Newman along with her
Senate chief of staff Nathan Barankin and pollster
David Binder sat down in the conference room
of the apartment building with Maya, Kamala's
brother-in-law Tony West and her husband Doug
Emhoff to discuss the decision. Should she go in all
guns blazing? What would it cost? How would it
impact their lives? There were innumerable issues to
consider – after all, Kamala had made up her mind

to enter the race for the post of the President of the United States.

The country's leading pollster and political observer David Binder had been roped in to do an in-depth analysis and present his conclusions to those closest to Kamala – and so he did.

Since Kamala was a Democrat, it meant that the competition up ahead would be tough from candidates on the same side, but her life experience and background as a prosecutor, along with her position on the issue of immigrants, could act as an advantage. But what about the finances? Everyone knew that deciding to run for President is one thing, and sustaining a presidential campaign is quite another. It was decided that with the kind of connections she had in Oakland, San Francisco, Silicon Valley and Los Angeles, Kamala probably had an edge when it came to raising money. It would not be a cakewalk, but it could be pulled off. No one was exuberant though, and everyone tried to remain humble and realistic about what lay ahead.

Then came the question of whether the timing was right for her. She had been in the Senate for less than two years. Shouldn't a presidential candidate work on building a more impressive record? Tony West elaborated on the cons of her running for the top post in the country. There would be an emotional and physical toll that would come with the campaign. Everyone would face scrutiny, including Kamala's stepchildren. What if they threw a party to promote her candidacy and nobody showed up? That would spell disaster for her standing. It could potentially derail her career and ruin the decades of work she had done. After an intensive two days of listing pros and cons, Kamala Harris, the politician who had sometimes been criticized for being excessively cautious had made up her mind. She was ready to take the plunge.

Over the next few months Kamala stepped up the staffing of the campaign team in a controlled and calculated manner. A space in Baltimore was quietly rented to function as the headquarters from where the campaign would be directed. Although she did not have a connection with the city in Maryland, having her base on the East Coast, closer to the epicentre of American politics, was important. As far as politics is concerned in the United States, news always travels from east to west, not vice versa. With this in mind she abandoned California for Baltimore, despite having a very strong base in the former.

The confirmation hearings for Supreme Court justice Brett Kavanaugh were scheduled to be held in the first week of September 2018, after which she was to hop on to the campaign trail. At this stage she was presenting stump speeches which would be used for candidates running in the 2018 midterms, many of them located in states significant to the Democratic presidential primary. In the fall and early winter of 2018, during committee hearings she questioned officials from the Trump administration about the treatment of pregnant refugees in custody at the border. She requested that the Department of Homeland Security reunite children separated from their parents. At the same time, she sowed the seeds of a legislation that required that Border Patrol and Immigrations and Customs Enforcement agents wear body cameras, and also contributed as one of the authors of an anti-lynching legislation passed by the Senate. In November 2018, she surveyed the destruction caused by the deadly wildfire now known as Camp Fire, which killed more than 85 people that season and devastated Paradise, a town in northern California.

Kamala was neck-deep in many activities and everything was going well, when some unexpected business came up in California. This was a troublesome and ill-timed news piece published in the *Sacramento Bee* in early December 2018. The report stated that in 2017, just after Kamala had been sworn in as senator, California attorney general Xavier Becerra had settled a sexual harassment claim against Larry Wallace, the director of the Division of Law Enforcement, for $400,000. Wallace was also part of Kamala's Senate staff. The settlement was a clear embarrassment for the senator and reflected badly on her role as a manager. Her aides presented an explanation – she did not know that the complaint had been filed, let alone that the case was up for a settlement. However, since the Division of Law Enforcement is a key component of the Department of Justice, with its director reporting to the attorney general, a post held by Kamala at the time, the explanation seemed rather unconvincing. Eventually, Wallace resigned from her Senate staff. He had been with her since the mid-2000s, from the time she was San Francisco's district attorney.

The nightmare now behind her, at the end of 2018, Kamala embarked on a journey to Afghanistan, visiting Kabul, Mazar-e Sharif and Kandahar. There she received briefings and met with American troops, diplomats and national security professionals to assess the situation. 'I was grateful to receive on-the-ground briefings on the state of the region and discuss how best to keep our country and our allies safe from the threat posed by terrorism,' she said in a statement on her return. 'I remain eager to find a political solution to the ongoing conflict in Afghanistan so we can bring US service members and national security professionals home,' she concluded. Previously, in 2017, as a member of the Senate Select Committee on Intelligence and the Homeland Security and Governmental Affairs Committee, Kamala had flown to Iraq to visit American troops fighting ISIS mercenaries. Till her visit to Afghanistan in 2018, Kamala had not announced that she would be running for President. A report published in the *San Francisco Chronicle* stated, 'The timing of the trip is likely to invite speculation about Harris' 2020 presidential ambitions. Harris is a former prosecutor and ex-California attorney general, and foreign policy is one area where she could be looking to bolster her credentials heading into a wide-open Democratic primary season.' This caused media curiosity to pique and conjectures began to float around. Publications such as the *New York Times, Washington Post* and others listed her in their year-end stories, speculating if she would run for President. Senators Cory Booker, Kirsten Gillibrand and Elizabeth Warren were also featured in these lists. Bernie Sanders was in the running, and Joe Biden was expected to enter the arena as well. CNN announced as many as 29 potential presidential candidates from the Democratic Party. Four of them were from California. The competition was heating up.

At this time, Kamala also had to arrange and channelize funds for her presidential campaign, in keeping with the American electoral convention that candidates running for political office must raise money for their campaign on their own in order to demonstrate the extent of support for them. There are laws concerning who can contribute to a campaign, how much they can contribute, and how those contributions must be reported. For instance, corporations, labour organizations and membership groups cannot contribute directly to federal campaigns. However, they can influence federal elections by creating political action committees, better known as PACs. These committees seek donations from members and associates to make campaign contributions or fund campaign activities such as advertising. Raising funds is a crucial part of the campaigning process as in the election dollars often equal votes. Kamala received a lot of support from women-led PACs, individual women donors as well as a sizeable sum from the Democratic strongholds in Hollywood and Silicon Valley. It helped that she was the first Democratic candidate from California to be on a presidential ticket in the modern political era. There was an added edge in her favour because California was at the time being ravaged by wildfires. The state would gain from many benefits if the President-elect was a representative from California.

Throughout the endless media speculations about her candidature, Kamala had remained tight-lipped about her decision. On a morning appearance on the ABC talk show *The View* on 9 January 2019 to host Whoopi Goldberg's direct query, Kamala retorted wittily, 'I'm pleased to announce on *The View* that I'm not ready to make my announcement.' The studio erupted in laughter. 'I'm very tempted,' she continued, once the mirth subsided, 'but I'm not yet ready.'

The announcement was finally made on another ABC talk show, *Good Morning America*, on 21 January 2019. 'The American people deserve to have somebody who is going to fight for them, who is going to see them, who will hear them, who will care about them, who will be concerned about their experience and will put them in front of self-interest,' she said.

The kick-off rally was scheduled for the following Sunday, 27 January, in Oakland. Her consultants used their experience of October 2007, when they had organized Hillary Clinton's California presidential campaign, drawing 14,000 people to downtown Oakland. They worked tirelessly to pull off an even more impressive event and engage a bigger crowd. Their efforts paid off. A whopping 20,000 people showed up at Oakland City Hall, which was decorated with American flags along with red, white and blue buntings draped all over the premises. Kamala started her address by talking about Martin Luther King, Jr., and reminded all those present that Shirley Chisholm had made her historic announcement as the first black woman running for President forty years earlier. Her speech, aimed to strike a chord with regular folk, was peppered with references to African American heroes. She revealed to her audience that she was born a stone's throw away at the Kaiser Permanente Hospital, and had worked in the Oakland courts as an Alameda County deputy district attorney. She told them how proud she had been when she stood in a courtroom and said for the first time: 'Kamala Harris. For the People.' That was her theme that day – For the People. It was meant to represent the foundation for her presidential run, to highlight inclusivity and welcome everyone with open arms, no matter what the age, colour, race or gender. The strategy was clear – get a headstart in the race, make a splash, display strength and, possibly, thin the field.

'I'm running to be President, of the people, by the people, and for all people,' she said.

The event was a runaway success. Trump, the man who is a big fan of big crowds, admitted in a *New York Times* interview that her Oakland event was 'the best opening so far'. Jackie Philips, the principal at Cole School in Oakland and Kamala's former teacher, was among those who attended the event. She had known her student as a teenager who was always ready to have fun, but also harboured a deep desire to make something of herself. Philips said she was 'proud beyond words'. It was a promising beginning at the state level. A national campaign was up next.

For the next few weeks Kamala would be seen at rallies at various locations – she was running around, but not in heels. In many ways, by being seen in Converse sneakers, she rewrote the rulebook on political style – she was the first presidential (and later vice presidential) candidate to do so. But the pairing of elegant power pearls with functional sneakers wasn't just for the campaign, she's always been partial to comfy footwear. 'I run through airports in my Converse sneakers,' she told TheCut. com. 'I have a whole collection of Chuck Taylors: a black leather pair, a white pair, I have the kind that don't lace, the kind that do lace, the kind I wear in the hot weather, the kind I wear in the cold weather, and the platform kind for when I'm wearing a pantsuit.'

After witnessing such a great start, within two weeks of announcing her candidacy, Fox News was quick to declare Kamala Harris as the front runner in the race for the main position in the White House. Although Joe Biden remained the prime candidate from the beginning to the end, Kamala too remained in the top tier, which meant a great deal of scrutiny.

While Maya, with her impressive résumé and experience with the Hillary Clinton presidential campaign, was chairing Kamala's campaign in the east, the majority of the team behind the strategy remained in San Francisco. 'She's invaluable,' Kamala said of Maya in a feature in the *Washington Post*. 'There's no amount of money I can pay her, so I pay her no amount of money.' According to a report in the *Independent*, 'Largely every facet of the Harris presidential campaign was touched by the younger Ms Harris – from soliciting donors to recruiting a diverse staff to even drafting policy initiatives the campaign would lead on.'

With all the favourable press she was receiving, it almost seemed like Kamala was invincible. However, competing factions and a few self-inflicted setbacks did some damage to the campaign. Observers pointed to Kamala's habit of avoiding reporters and often presenting ambiguous positions on issues as factors that worked against her. For instance, while Kamala had publicly claimed that she was against the decriminalization of marijuana, in July 2019 she co-sponsored a bill to federally decriminalize marijuana and legalize its commercial sale. The legislation was called the Marijuana Opportunity Reinvestment and Expungement Act, or the MORE Act. This appeared to her supporters as an inconsistency on her part. Another matter that vexed some of her admirers was her diffident stand on the decriminalizing of prostitution between consenting adults – in particular because they knew of the fearless stance she had adopted in 2016, when she announced the arrest of Carl Ferrer, the CEO of Backpage.com, a website that offered 'escort services' under the garb of being a classifieds listing site. Ferrer was charged with pimping, pimping of minors and the conspiracy to commit pimping, and his website was ultimately forced to shut down its adult section. At the time Kamala had been commended highly for her fast and decisive action on the protection of rights of children and women, making her later timid response to a similar issue unexpected and disappointing.

Kamala realized the hard way that with the spotlight perennially on her, every word she uttered during the presidential race came with consequences. In February 2019, an interview featured on the Breakfast Club podcast led to another controversy. On the podcast Kamala had casually told the host that she had smoked marijuana in college, adding, 'Half my family's from Jamaica. Are you kidding me?' It left her father, Stanford professor Donald Harris, a proud Jamaican, not the least bit pleased. He wrote in his blog that his deceased grandmothers and parents 'must be turning in their graves right now to see their family's name, reputation and proud Jamaican identity being connected, in any way, jokingly or not, with the fraudulent stereotype of a pot-smoking joy-seeker and in the pursuit of identity politics'. He removed the post soon enough, but by then it had been widely reported on and a significant amount of damage done to Kamala's reputation.

Trouble began to emerge on other fronts too.

Contrary to what everyone in Kamala's immediate circle had counted on, fundraising too was fast becoming a concern for the campaign staff. Coming from California and competing in three statewide elections had not given Kamala the edge everyone had thought it would. Despite her remarkable kick-off in Oakland, the total amount raised in the first quarter of 2019 was $12 million, which was not much to write home about. Senator Barack Obama, in comparison, had raised $25 million in the first quarter after announcing his candidacy, and that had been more than a decade ago, in 2007.

Kamala was also not garnering as much attention as had been expected. She was up against strong women contenders, such as Massachusetts senator Elizabeth Warren, Minnesota senator Amy Klobuchar and New York senator Kirsten Gillibrand, who were tough competition. Former South Bend Mayor Pete Buttigieg was also fighting for the limelight and capturing the imagination of newly eligible and first-time voters who wanted to see a younger president at the helm of affairs. He stood out as the only candidate who, in his own words, was 'the only left-handed Maltese-American-Episcopalian-gay-millennial war veteran in the race'. Educated in Harvard and a Rhodes Scholar, Buttigieg seemed to be turning into a formidable opponent, drawing away voters, including several in California that Kamala might have been counting on. And then there was Joe Biden to worry about as well. The main issue, however, was that Kamala's campaign did not have a clear definition in terms of the reason for her being in strong contention in the race – besides prosecuting the case against Trump's tyrannous regime, that is. Unfortunately, in politics, fighting to defeat someone is never considered a good reason to fight. She needed to bring something more to the table. She needed to establish what exactly she hoped to achieve if she was elected President.

Soon enough, she got a fantastic opportunity to turn the race around and prove the worth of her candidacy beyond debate. The chance arrived with the first Democratic presidential debate that took place on 27 June 2019. It was against Joe Biden on the big stage at the Adrienne Arsht Center for the Performing Arts in Miami, Florida. 'I would like to speak on the issue of race,' she began. Starting gently, she stated that she didn't believe Biden was a racist, her words clearly implying that he could probably harbour racist leanings. The debate proceeded from that point, gradually rising in tempo, and then, an hour into it, she attacked her opponent quite directly on the issue of race, bringing up his association decades earlier with segregationist senators and his efforts to curb the bussing scheme in order to prevent school desegregation.

'[I]t was hurtful to hear you talk about the reputations of two United States senators who built their reputations and career on the segregation of race in this country,' she said, addressing Biden. 'And it was not only that, but you also worked with them to oppose bussing. And, you know, there was a little girl in California who was part of the second class to integrate her public schools, and she was bussed to school every day. And that little girl was me,' she said. Her fearless attack on the leading favourite in the presidential election on the crucial issue of race made one thing crystal clear. She would not retreat from the fight and she was running to win. Almost immediately, her fundraising graph heightened, giving her a boost in polling. Journalists were in awe of her and established that she was the clear winner in the first debate. However, the elation as well as the polling spike was short-lived.

The first debate sparked controversy in the days to come, with Kamala's supporters and critics in contention over whether the meticulously rehearsed attack was politically sensible or a deliberate hit below the belt. Was it relevant to bring up something that had happened so far back in the past? Was it Kamala's way of resuscitating life into a dying campaign? On the other hand, it was clear to all who had witnessed the exchange that had Kamala Harris not put herself out there as a personification of a multicultural America where race was an issue that could not be stopped from being discussed, she would not deserve to be in the running.

Meanwhile, the attack on Biden had taken him completely by surprise. 'I thought we were friends, and I hope we still will be,' he said on the *Tom Joyner Morning Show* when asked about the debate. Biden also mentioned in that interview that when in 2016 Kamala had requested him to come to the California Democratic Convention in San Jose to endorse her candidacy for the United States Senate, he had done so. His attendance and heartfelt speech had fortified the Democratic Party's endorsement of Kamala over Loretta Sanchez, her opponent at the time.

In the general election, Kamala's background as a prosecutor, someone who had put people behind bars for their wicked deeds, would be a strong pitch. However, in the primary stages, she was under the scanner, being challenged and scrutinized by social justice activists who questioned whether she was indeed the 'progressive' prosecutor she had presented herself to be.

On 17 January 2019, Lara Bazelon, an associate professor at the University of San Francisco School of Law, criticized her in an opinion piece published in the *New York Times*. 'Time after time, when progressives urged her to embrace criminal justice reforms as a district attorney and then the state's attorney general, Ms Harris opposed them or stayed silent. Most troubling, Ms Harris fought tooth and nail to uphold wrongful convictions that had been secured through official misconduct that included evidence tampering, false testimony and the suppression of crucial information by prosecutors.' The piece tore the very fabric of her campaign, though it did not dismantle it completely.

Congresswoman Tulsi Gabbard of Hawaii, picking up on the theme, was particularly ruthless in her attack in the second Democratic presidential primary debate. During the debate held in Detroit at the end of July, Gabbard had proclaimed that Kamala had 'put over 1,500 people in jail for marijuana violations', and failed to probe evidence that might have absolved a death row inmate. She said this with reference to the Kevin Cooper case. Cooper was convicted of killing a couple, their ten-year-old daughter and their daughter's friend, an eleven-year-old boy, in Chino Hills, California. The couple's eight-year-old son, who had been present in their home when the incident occurred, had survived the attack with a cut to the neck. His testimony, therefore, was of paramount importance. After initially suggesting that three people had visited the house on the day of the attack, looking for work, he later testified against Cooper, identifying him as the sole assailant. According to an ABC news report, 'The question of Harris' actions surfaced later – when Cooper and his lawyers asked the state to approve additional DNA testing, which they argued could exonerate him. Harris' team did not take up the case, and evidence from the crime scene was never re-examined while Harris held state office.' Later, in a *New York Times* post in 2018, Kamala said, 'As a firm believer in DNA testing, I hope the Governor and the state will allow for such testing in the case of Kevin Cooper.' However, it was too late for her to act on her statement and effect change as she had by then moved on from the position and was a senator.

Though taken out of context and not really relevant to the debate in question, the issue being brought up was unexpected and embarrassing for Kamala, especially on a stage crowded with ten candidates. Kamala could not give a fitting reply. Things went further downhill when she appeared on CNN in conversation with journalist-anchor Anderson Cooper. Instead of taking an affirmative position or presenting any clarifications with regard to Gabbard's accusations, she said, 'This is going to sound immodest, but obviously I'm a top-tier candidate and so I did expect that I'd be on the stage and take some hits tonight, because there are a lot of people who are trying to make the stage for the next debate… Especially, when people are at zero or one per cent or whatever she [Gabbard] might be at, so I did expect to take some hits tonight.' In implying that Gabbard did not have as much at stake as she did, and had thus chosen to attack Kamala, Kamala came across as pompous and wanting to belittle her opponent.

Whatever the cause, by the beginning of November 2019 Kamala's campaign had begun to fizzle out due to a lack of funds and her crumbling operations were making it to news pieces in various publications. On 29 November the *New York Times* presented a nearly 3,000-word deconstruction of the campaign under the headline 'How Kamala Harris's Campaign Unraveled'. It stated, 'The 2020 Democratic field has been defined by its turbulence, with some contenders rising, others dropping out and two more jumping in just this month. Yet there is only one candidate who rocketed to the top tier and then plummeted in early state polls to the low single digits: Ms Harris.' It was common knowledge by now that one of her main consultants, Juan Rodriguez, was taking the sack, and that was just a hint of how things had become inside the campaign. Frequent disagreements had begun to ensue between Maya and turned out, while the younger campaign workers wanted a more liberal approach to the campaign, causing a generational rift. The internal drama had become unmanageable. Campaign workers who lost their jobs due to money running out were sneering as they made their way out.

Realizing she had no significant funds left, Kamala decided to opt out of the race after deliberating with her team. By taking this decision early on, she saved herself the awkwardness of losing big in the Iowa caucus and, worse, in her home state, California. Her name would now not appear on California's primary ballot to be held on 3 March 2020. It was a smart move as polls showed she was all set to lose California. A loss in her own state would not only have been disconcerting and disheartening, but would have also raised questions about her viability as a candidate in future elections.

The presidential campaign done with, Kamala resumed the work for which she had been elected: representing her state in the United States Senate. Returning to the life she had had before embarking on her presidential campaign, she engaged herself in meaningful work, introducing as many as thirty-three bills and resolutions. These bills, however, got little or no media attention. Some of them sought to address issues specific to California, such as reinstating and increasing access to public lands, and taking up measures to counter pollution in the Tijuana river located at the California–Mexico border. She also took up issues that she had raised on the campaign trail, such as environmental justice bills to safeguard those belonging to underprivileged communities from the deadly effects of industrial pollution. Also on her agenda was funding research into alternatives to chemicals used in consumer products including cosmetics. This was specifically in the interest of protecting women who worked in salons frequently coming into contact with chemicals on the job. Earlier, specific issues such as this would not be taken up seriously in the Senate, but used more as umbrella issues to decorate legislative packages.

At the beginning of 2020, when practically the entire world was in the throes of the Covid-19 pandemic, Kamala's response to it was quick and decisive. She called for a slew of changes aimed at protecting American citizens, including federal laws barring landlords from evicting renters and providing 18 months for the latter to make up for missed rent payments, and unveiled legislation that banned foreclosures for a year. Kamala signed on a bill led by Senator Bernie Sanders that aimed to provide face masks to all Americans at no cost. She also put forward proposals to freeze rent increases, eliminate penalties and late fees and prevent landlords from reporting unpaid rent to credit reporting agencies. Further, she co-sponsored a bill that would allow Medicaid programmes to pay for hospitalization, drugs and vaccines for people suffering from Covid-19 who were uninsured. In this uncertain election year, Kamala was a Democrat in a Republican-controlled Senate, in which she had bent over backwards to be a presidential nominee. This meant that the chances of the bills she had proposed winning passage were meagre. However, each bill was a testament to the kind of issues she could address if she got the opportunity.

Kamala might have let go of her campaign, but she had held on steadfastly to her dream – and now it seemed that the universe was aligning to make it come true. On 11 August 2020, a Tuesday, fellow presidential candidate Joseph Biden connected with Kamala on a Zoom call to ask her if she was interested in being his running mate. 'You ready to go to work?' he asked breezily. 'Oh my God. I'm so ready to go to work,' she answered. To Kamala and her team Biden's offer came as a surprise considering their last encounter at the debate on 27 June 2019. Joe Biden's wife, Dr Jill Biden, had especially not taken it well and had called the attack on her husband on the issue of race 'a punch to the gut'.

Not that Kamala had not been aware that she was on the list of potentials. When word had got out that Biden had decided to select a woman as his running mate and he announced the same on 15 March 2020 while making his way to accepting his Democratic nomination, Kamala had realized there was damage control to be done with regard to the way the debate between Biden and her had unfolded. So, on *The Late Show* with Stephen Colbert in June, Harris offered a rather nervous explanation on why she had challenged Biden over race. 'It was a debate. The whole reason – literally, it was a debate. It was called a debate.' When Colbert asked her about her reaction to being a likely choice for Biden's running mate, she said, 'I'd be honoured, if asked, and I'm honoured to be a part of the conversation. Honestly, let me just tell you something. I will do everything in my power, wherever I am, to help Joe Biden win.' While she did not campaign or lobby around for the position, Kamala knew that she was in the running. Kamala also ensured Biden knew that in case differences arose on issues of race and criminal justice, which she was passionate about, Biden's views would be prioritized. Among the black women being considered by Biden's team, Kamala had the advantage of being the only one with the experience of winning major statewide contests and running in a national campaign.

Biden had always admired her insightful and fearless approach to all political matters. His late son, Beau, who had passed away due to brain cancer in 2015, had also had a high opinion of Kamala, which majorly influenced Biden's choice. Beau was impressed with her body of work, particularly that as a state attorney general she had challenged the banks in 2011 and 2012 to help victims of foreclosure. 'There is no one's opinion I valued more than Beau's and I'm proud to have Kamala standing with me on this campaign,' Biden said after the selection.

The timing of the Black Lives Matter movement may also have been a key factor for Biden to consider taking on the half-Indian, half-Jamaican Kamala for a running mate – it was time for some diversity to be represented in the White House. The Black Lives Matter movement had started as a protest against police atrocities on black citizens across the United States. On 25 May 2020, Minneapolis resident George Floyd died pinned under the knee of a police officer for eight minutes and forty-six seconds, begging to be allowed to breathe. The police had recklessly disregarded his pleas. His offence was buying a pack of cigarettes with a counterfeit $20 bill. Just two months earlier, police in Louisville, Kentucky, had mistakenly shot and killed Breonna Taylor, an innocent 26-year-old emergency room technician, while she was in her bed. The police claimed they thought they were raiding the home of drug dealers. Breonna Taylor's senseless killing was still fresh in the nation's memory when the George Floyd incident occurred, fuelling the campaign further. After Breonna Taylor's death, Kamala had taken to Twitter to demand the arrest of the police officers involved; after the George Floyd incident too she had not wasted any time. In an op-ed for *Cosmopolitan*, she wrote, 'Let's speak the truth: People are protesting because Black people have been treated as less than human in America. Because our country has never fully addressed the systemic racism that has plagued [us] since its earliest days. It is the duty of every American to fix. No longer can [we] wait on the sidelines, hoping for incremental change. In times like this, silence is complicity.' Five days later, she put on a mask and marched straight to the White House to join the protests there.

In many ways, Kamala is a sound choice for a running mate. She complements Joe Biden in a unique way. Biden is the oldest man ever to be elected President of the United States. Kamala, on the other hand, is nearly two decades younger and can offer a fresh, younger perspective on things. Apart from the generational balance, she also brings an ideological and racial stability to the Democratic ticket. Her close contacts with women in the Democratic Party, people of colour and Hollywood celebrities also comes as an added advantage for the former vice president as it can help her to raise funds. Democratic donor Katie McGrath, co-chief executive of production company Bad Robot and wife of celebrated director J.J. Abrams, told the *Wall Street Journal*, 'When you think about balancing a ticket, she brings a lot of the qualities that I think are important in 2020.' The Hollywood power couple have been her long-time supporters. Upon her selection as Biden's running mate, Kamala hosted over two dozen virtual fundraisers, with and without donors from the entertainment industry.

In an opinion piece published on CNN.com, Sarah Elizabeth Cupp, CNN's political commentator and the host of *SE Cupp: Unfiltered*, suggested that Biden had to pair with Kamala in order to defeat Donald Trump. The viability of the choice was very high as all the other prospective candidates came with 'major baggage or alienating qualities'. She also highlighted the authenticity factor. 'With Harris, Biden has put his money where his mouth is. It's one thing to say you care about ending racism, it's another to put a woman on the ticket who will make it her priority. If he truly empowers her to do just that, to have a voice on those issues that even overpowers and outshines his own, it could go a long way toward reassuring many Americans on the left and the right, young and old, White and Black, that an older White guy is truly interested in helping to usher in a new era of racial justice.'

According to a report on BBC.com, Gil Duran, a communications director for Kamala in 2013, who has criticized her run for the presidential nomination, commented, 'It is a big reversal of fortune for Kamala Harris. Many people didn't think she had the discipline and focus to ascend to a position in the White House so quickly... Although people knew she had ambition and star potential. It was always clear that she had the raw talent.'

After considering twenty candidates for the job, and eventually narrowing the list down to eleven, Biden was convinced that Kamala was the one. The vetting committee said in a statement published in CBS News on 12 August 2020 that Kamala Harris 'would be the best governing partner to help him lead our country out of the chaos created by Donald Trump'.

Within a few hours of her name being announced, Biden's campaign raised over $10 million. His decision had worked like a charm.

9

THE RACE TO THE FINISH LINE

'No matter who you voted for, I will strive to be the Vice President that Joe was to President Obama – loyal, honest and prepared, waking up every day thinking of you and your families.'

– **Kamala Harris**, Instagram post

AND NOW IT WAS SHOWTIME.

The months of hard work that had gone into Kamala's presidential campaign had not been a total waste. Kamala had emerged as a strong voice – a voice of the people and for the people. But, more than anything else, she was associated with grit. By putting her on his ticket, presidential nominee Joe Biden had pulled her back into the spotlight. Having served as vice president of the United States for almost a decade, from 2009 to 2017, Biden knew what he was looking for – someone who had all the trappings to fulfil the role he had held for such a long time. 'Long before Joe Biden would choose Harris as his running mate, he stressed his wish to tap someone who would be a partner in governing and campaigning,' stated an article in NBC News.

On 12 August 2020, a day after announcing Kamala as the vice presidential nominee, the two made their first public appearance together to endorse their campaigns. 'As they appeared together [on] Wednesday for the first time as running mates, Biden and Harris reflected on the significance of the moment,' the AP News report added. Biden said, 'This morning, all across the nation, little girls woke up – especially little black and brown girls, who so often feel overlooked and undervalued in their communities. But today, today, just maybe, they're seeing themselves for the first time in a new way.' On 18 August, the second night of the 2020 Democratic National Convention, the party officially nominated Biden for the President's post. This made him the first non-incumbent vice president to be nominated for the post of President after Walter Mondale in 1984. It also made Kamala the first Indian American and the first female African American to be nominated for the vice president's position.

Accepting his nomination two nights later, Biden delivered an acceptance speech that was very well received by the media. He criticized the Trump administration for its segregationist politics. 'The current President has cloaked America in darkness for much too long. Too much anger. Too much fear. Too much division. Here and now, I give you my word: If you entrust me with the Presidency, I will draw on the best of us, not the worst. I will be an ally of the light, not of the darkness. It's time for us, for We the People, to come together.' He also brought up President Trump's inability to handle the coronavirus crisis and the economic emergency the country was facing as a result: '5 million Americans infected with COVID-19. More than 170,000 Americans have died.'

On his choice of the vice presidential nomination, he said, 'I won't have to do it alone. Because I will have a great Vice President at my side. Senator Kamala Harris. She is a powerful voice for this nation. Her story is the American story. She knows about all the obstacles thrown in the way of so many in our country. Women, black women, black Americans, South Asian Americans, immigrants, the left-out and left-behind.

'But she's overcome every obstacle she's ever faced. No one's been tougher on the big banks or the gun lobby. No one's been tougher in calling out this current administration for its extremism, its failure to follow the law, and its failure to simply tell the truth.'

In contrast, responding to Kamala's nomination as the vice presidential candidate, Trump described her as 'meanest' and 'most horrible'. This was a surprise considering that as a private citizen, and before becoming the President, Trump and his daughter had made donations towards Kamala's campaigns for the post of attorney general. He was clearly miffed at the prospect of a black woman, a black woman who had ripped his administration apart in the Senate, coming into a position of such power. During the last few weeks of the campaign, Trump also shifted the focus from Biden to Kamala as polls started swaying against him. From mocking her name to making fun of her laughter and calling her 'incompetent', he made every effort to belittle her. 'She will not be the first woman President...you can't let that happen,' he told the crowds during an election rally in Pennsylvania. 'I said, "Is there something wrong with her?" She kept laughing at very, you know, serious questions.' But Kamala was hardly perturbed. She continued laughing her signature, hearty laughter all the way to the big win.

With the former President Barack Obama backing the Biden–Harris campaign with great gusto, the duo seemed to be set for a win. When Kamala was announced as the vice presidential nominee, Obama tweeted: 'I've known Senator @ KamalaHarris for a long time. She is more than prepared for the job. She's spent her career defending our Constitution and fighting for folks who need a fair shake. This is a good day for our country. Now let's go win this thing.' Obama was sure that his former vice president, with whom he shared a great relationship, would also prove to be adept at handling the Covid crisis and would not mess things up like Trump had, he said at a drive-in rally at Orlando, Florida. 'He's not going to call scientists idiots. He's not going to host a superspreader event at the White House, and then take it on a tour all across the country!'

With the pandemic hitting hard, the presidential campaigns this time around were a little different from earlier ones. Large, traditional campaigns teeming with people would not be the norm. Several of the scheduled primaries were also postponed, while a lot of the action moved to the virtual stage.

Nevertheless, there was work to be done, and there wasn't much time.

The first presidential debate was organized at the Cleveland Clinic on 29 September 2020 between Trump and Biden, and moderated by Chris Wallace of Fox News. It was now time for the vice presidential debate. Kamala Harris and Mike Pence took each other on on 7 October 2020 with the Washington bureau chief of *USA Today*, Susan Page, donning the role of moderator. The debate was largely seen as a civil exchange, unlike the debate between Biden and Trump (a news portal had reported 71 interruptions from Trump's end and 22 from Biden's). Kamala only interrupted approximately half as often as Pence. A moment that was much applauded during the debate, especially by feminists on social media, was when Kamala responded to Mike Pence who was interrupting her, by simply smiling and saying, 'Mr Vice President, I'm speaking… If you don't mind letting me finish, then we can have a conversation.' Overlooking the moderator's attempts at asking him to be mindful of the two-minute limit, Pence also continued to frequently speak beyond his allotted time. A poll of registered voters by CNN found that

59 per cent of the voters thought Kamala had won, while 38 per cent thought the winner was Pence.

According to a coverage and analysis report of the vice presidential debate on the BBC, 'Ms Harris was "clearly prepared" for interruptions, says Deborah Tannen, a linguistics professor at Georgetown University and expert in gender differences in language use. She came across as "respectful" by saying "Mr Vice President", while "I'm speaking" was not accusatory in the way "stop interrupting me" would have been. Clearly her challenge throughout the whole debate was to avoid coming across as aggressive.' For obvious reasons, she might have been mindful of the reviews garnered during the grilling sessions of the Trump administration officials in the Senate. Knowing the stakes were so high she wisely steered clear of tags such as 'aggressive' and 'disrespectful'.

Soon enough, it was time for the final countdown, with only one month to go between the campaigning and elections. With just three days to go for the elections, at the fag end of the campaign trail, an incident in Texas created some controversy. On 31 October 2020, a Joe Biden campaign bus was on the way from San Antonio to Austin. The bus, carrying former state senator Wendy Davis and many campaign staffers, was followed along Interstate 35 by a host of cars, some of their passengers waving Donald Trump flags. As a result, the Biden campaign team had to cancel two planned events in Austin. On the next day it was announced that the incident would not be taken lightly and that the FBI was being brought in to investigate it. At a rally, Trump went on to condemn the FBI's decision to get involved. He took to Twitter to express his criticism. 'In my opinion, these patriots did nothing wrong. Instead, the FBI & Justice should be investigating the terrorists, anarchists, and agitators of Antifa, who run around burning down our Democrat-run cities and hurting our people!'

Biden's list of endorsements was a long one – almost every Democratic candidate who had quit the presidential race had backed him. The list included the names of some rebel Republicans who were fed up of Trump's waywardness. Naturally, the opinion polls reflected the nationwide support for

Biden as presidential candidate. In general, opinion polls conducted in 2020 indicated that Biden had the upper hand over Trump nationally in general election matchups.

A national poll taken in the beginning of August showed Biden to be ahead by 3 per cent. An Iowa poll concluded that Trump was leading Biden by 48 per cent to 45 per cent, six points lower than what Trump had won the state with back in 2016. After Kamala came into the picture, as many as three national polls showed Biden polling ahead of Trump. According to Fox News, Biden was leading Trump 49 per cent–42 per cent, while NBC/*Wall Street Journal* showed a bigger margin of 50 per cent–41 per cent. A poll analysis published on CNN's news portal showed interesting and contradictory results, warning everyone to not just go by the polls. 'The result of the 2016 outcome for this cycle is that the general public doesn't buy the polling showing Biden clearly ahead. They think Trump is going to win,' stated the report. 'A Pew Research Center poll... demonstrates what's going on quite well. The poll had Biden up by 8 points over Trump, very similar to the average and the Ipsos poll discussed earlier. Yet, the same poll found that Americans believed by a

51% to 46% margin that Trump would defeat Biden in the election. (Among voters, it was a tighter 50% to 48% spread in favor of Trump.) The poll indicates that voters either believe the race will shift back to Trump or that the polling is wrong,' the report concluded. It was clear now that anything could happen. Trump could not be written off just yet.

A *Washington Post*/ABC News poll conducted later in September showed Biden's and Kamala's lead to be 53 per cent–43 per cent. That was a good margin to achieve. These numbers went on to get better, with NBC News/*Wall Street Journal* reporting Biden leading 53 per cent–39 per cent. On 2 October, Trump announced on Twitter that he had been infected with the coronavirus. Some called it a move to get voter sympathy. On 7 October, with less than a month to go for election day on 3 November, a CNN poll showed Biden leading by 16 per cent and a week ahead, in the *Opinium Research*/*Guardian* poll, the margin was 17 per cent.

'We did it, we did it, Joe. You're going to be the next President of the United States!' Kamala posted a video of her on 7 November, dressed in a tracksuit, probably just out of a workout and holding her earphones in one hand, making a call to

Biden. The hearty laughter with which she greeted the President-elect during the once-in-a-lifetime congratulatory phone call showed that sparkling wit and humour was as much a part of her personality as grit. Trump, Jr. had once tweeted, 'Why is Kamala Harris the only person that laughs at her jokes... always way too long and way too hard? The most disingenuous person in politics...after Hillary.' He had included a video clip of Kamala laughing after a reporter asked her, 'How do you describe yourself?' Kamala's famous response to the President's son had made the headlines: 'You wouldn't know a joke if one raised you.' Twitter went into overdrive that day, with users appreciating her sassy reply with a simple burn. That had been about a year earlier, in 2019. On the day of the results, Twitter would come alive again with congratulatory messages pouring in from politicians, celebrities, sportspersons and the common folk who had made their choice. They were now safe in the knowledge that the hearty laughter common to both the Harris sisters would be heard daily in the White House.

World leaders joined in the elation by taking to various social media platforms to congratulate the duo. In a tweet, the prime minister of the United

Kingdom, Boris Johnson, said, 'Congratulations to Joe Biden on his election as President of the United States and to Kamala Harris on her historic achievement. The US is our most important ally and I look forward to working closely together on our shared priorities, from climate change to trade and security.' Indian Prime Minister Narendra Modi tweeted: 'Heartiest congratulations, Kamala Harris! Your success is pathbreaking, and a matter of immense pride not just for your chittis, but also for all Indian Americans. I am confident that the vibrant India–US ties will get even stronger with your support and leadership.' Interestingly, reports suggest that Kamala has been vocal against several issues of relevance to India, such as human rights violations in Kashmir after the calling down of Article 370. In a press conference in October 2019 she had said, 'We have to remind the Kashmiris that they are not alone in the world. We are keeping a track of the situation. There is a need to intervene if the situation demands [it].' It remains to be seen what will play out between the current governments on the issue.

Also congratulating the duo were celebrities from all walks of life.

Gwyneth Paltrow shared a picture of herself with Kamala Harris on Instagram, saying, 'A momentous day for women all around the globe as @kamalaharris makes history. Congratulations Madame Vice President.'

Michael Jordan also took to Instagram sharing a picture of the winning duo, saying, 'Let's celebrate President @joebiden and VP @KamalaHarris...and get down to work. #46 Justice was on the ballot. But now it's on the table. Let the negotiations begin.'

Oprah Winfrey, remembering Maya Angelou on the occasion, tweeted, 'And so we RISE as Maya would remind us. Character rises. Decency rises. The Soul of America gets a reset. And it starts now: #BidenHarris.'

'Congratulations to President-Elect Biden and Vice President-Elect Harris. Thank you to the election officials and campaign workers who worked tirelessly to ensure a record number of Americans could cast a ballot and have it counted during such a challenging time for our country,' Bill Gates said on Twitter. He also added in a thread to his Tweet, 'I look forward to working with the new administration and leaders on both sides in Congress on getting the surging pandemic under control, engaging partners around the world on issues like poverty and climate change, and addressing issues of inequality and opportunity at home.'

Compliments also poured in from Bollywood, with actress Priyanka Chopra leading the way. Sharing a photo of the news showing on her television screen on Instagram, she said, 'America spoke in record-breaking numbers and the verdict is in... every vote counts. I applaud everyone who voted in what was such a powerful display of how a democracy should function. It was amazing to witness this election in the US. Congrats to the President Elect @joebiden and Vice President-elect @kamalaharris, the first woman VP! Dream Big girls! Anything can happen!! #DemocracyRocks Congratulations America.'

Messages arrived from prominent political figures in America, 'I could not be prouder to congratulate our President, Joe Biden and our First Lady, Jill Biden. I also couldn't be prouder to congratulate Kamala Harris and Doug Emhoff for Kamala's groundbreaking election as our next Vice President,' said former President Barack Obama. Hillary Clinton, who was Trump's main threat in the election of 2016, stated, 'It's a history-making ticket, a repudiation of Trump, and a new page for America. Thank you to everyone who helped make this happen. Onward, together.'

In his victory speech, on 7 November, Biden had thanked his family and embraced his vice president's as well, saying, 'Kamala, Doug – like it or not – you're family. You've become honorary Bidens and there's no way out.' Kamala's take on their win was as decisive as it was hopeful: 'This election is about so much more than @JoeBiden or me. It's about the soul of America and our willingness to fight for it. We have a lot of work ahead of us. Let's get started.' Come 20 January 2021, the Biden–Harris duo will take their oath on the steps of the Capitol in Washington, DC, and all of the United States and the world will look forward to the dawn of a new era.

10

THE FIRST OF MANY

'That's why breaking those barriers is worth it. As much as anything else, it is also to create that path for those who will come after us.'

– **Kamala Harris**, in a lecture at Spelman College, Atlanta, Georgia

THE NIGHT OF 7 NOVEMBER 2020 WAS A BEAUTIFUL Saturday night in Wilmington, Delaware.

At the age of 56, Kamala Harris delivered her speech as the first woman, the first African American and the first South Asian to ascend to the second highest office in the United States. She stood out in an all-white Carolina Herrera pant-suit, her signature pearls, and a black mask, with her Converse sneakers traded in for beige pumps. The vice president-elect of the United States had lived up to her mother's words, 'You may be the first to do many things, but make sure you are not the last.'

To those watching in anticipation, the first speech Kamala had delivered as the Democratic nominee for the post came to mind. 'To everyone keeping up the fight, you are doing something,'

Kamala had said. 'You are the reason I know we are going to bring our country closer to realizing its great promise. But to do it, we'll need to work, organize, and vote like never before, because we need more than a victory on November third. We need a mandate that proves that the past few years do not represent who we are or who we aspire to be.' Her words instilled in those listening to her a sense of empowerment. It was no wonder then that the streets were filled with women as she addressed the nation, women of all ages and colour, to cheer their nation's newest role model. It was a remarkable moment. The members of the audience had not expected to be moved to tears, but they were.

'Good evening,' she greeted the crowd, before she went on to deliver a rousing speech.

Congressman John Lewis, before his passing, wrote: 'Democracy is not a state. It is an act.'

And what he meant was that America's democracy is not guaranteed.

It is only as strong as our willingness to fight for it, to guard it and never take it for granted.

And protecting our democracy takes struggle.

It takes sacrifice. There is joy in it and there is progress.

Because 'We the People' have the power to build a better future.

And when our very democracy was on the ballot in this election, with the very soul of America at stake, and the world watching, you ushered in a new day for America.

To our campaign staff and volunteers, this extraordinary team, thank you for bringing more people than ever before into the democratic process and for making this victory possible.

To the poll workers and election officials across our country who have worked tirelessly to make sure every vote is counted, our nation owes you a debt of gratitude as you have protected the integrity of our democracy.

And to the American people who make up our beautiful country, thank you for turning out in record numbers to make your voices heard.

I know times have been challenging, especially the last several months.

The grief, sorrow, and pain. The worries and the struggles.

But we've also witnessed your courage, your resilience, and the generosity of your spirit.

For four years, you marched and organized for equality and justice, for our lives, and for our planet.

And then, you voted. You delivered a clear message.

You chose hope, unity, decency, science, and, yes, truth.

You chose Joe Biden as the next President of the United States of America.

Joe is a healer. A uniter. A tested and steady hand.

A person whose own experience of loss gives him a sense of purpose that will help us, as a nation, reclaim our own sense of purpose.

And a man with a big heart who loves with abandon.

It's his love for Jill, who will be an incredible first lady.

It's his love for Hunter, Ashley, his grandchildren, and the entire Biden family.

And while I first knew Joe as Vice President, I really got to know him as the father who loved Beau, my dear friend, who we remember here today.

To my husband Doug, our children Cole and Ella, my sister Maya, and our whole family, I love you all more than I can express.

We are so grateful to Joe and Jill for welcoming our family into theirs on this incredible journey.

And to the woman most responsible for my presence here today, my mother, Shyamala Gopalan Harris, who is always in our hearts.

When she came here from India at the age of 19, maybe she didn't quite imagine this moment.

But she believed so deeply in an America where a moment like this is possible.

So, I'm thinking about her and about the generations of women, black women.

Asian, White, Latina, and Native American

women throughout our nation's history who have paved the way for this moment tonight.

Women who fought and sacrificed so much for equality, liberty, and justice for all, including the black women, who are too often overlooked, but so often prove that they are the backbone of our democracy.

All the women who worked to secure and protect the right to vote for over a century: 100 years ago with the 19th Amendment, 55 years ago with the Voting Rights Act, and now, in 2020, with a new generation of women in our country who cast their ballots and continued the fight for their fundamental right to vote and be heard.

Tonight, I reflect on their struggle, their determination and the strength of their vision, to see what can be unburdened by what has been, I stand on their shoulders.

And what a testament it is to Joe's character that he had the audacity to break one of the most substantial barriers that exists in our country and select a woman as his vice president.

But while I may be the first woman in this office, I won't be the last.

Because every little girl watching tonight sees that this is a country of possibilities.

And to the children of our country, regardless of your gender, our country has sent you a clear message:

Dream with ambition, lead with conviction, and see yourself in a way that others might not see you, simply because they've never seen it before.

And we will applaud you every step of the way.

To the American people:

No matter who you voted for, I will strive to be the Vice President that Joe was to President Obama, loyal, honest, and prepared, waking up every day thinking of you and your families. Because now is when the real work begins.

The hard work. The necessary work. The good work.

The essential work to save lives and beat this pandemic.

To rebuild our economy so it works for working people.

To root out systemic racism in our justice system and society.

To combat the climate crisis.

To unite our country and heal the soul of our nation.

The road ahead will not be easy.

But America is ready. And so are Joe and I.

We have elected a President who represents the best in us.

A leader the world will respect and our children can look up to.

A commander-in-chief who will respect our troops and keep our country safe.

And a President for all Americans.

It is now my great honor to introduce the President-elect of the United States of America, Joe Biden...

MILESTONES IN KAMALA HARRIS'S LIFE

1964   Born to Shyamala and Donald Harris in Oakland, California, on 20 October.

1981   Graduated from Westmount High School in Westmount, Quebec, Canada. Kamala's mother worked as a researcher and teacher in Montreal, Quebec, for a couple of years. Her parents had divorced by then.

1986   Graduated from Howard University in Washington, DC, with a degree in political science and economics. While at Howard, she also interned as a mailroom clerk at the office of California senator Alan Cranston.

1989   Graduated with a Juris Doctor from University of California Hastings College of Law. She served as the president of its chapter of the Black Law Students Association.

1990   Admitted to the State Bar of California in June. In the same year, she was hired as deputy district attorney in Alameda County, California.

1994   California assembly speaker Willie Brown appointed her to the state Unemployment Insurance Appeals Board. She was later appointed to the California Medical Assistance Commission.

1998   Moved to San Francisco to join the San Francisco district attorney's office as assistant district attorney. District Attorney Terence Hallinan put her in charge of the Career Criminal Division.

2000   Quit the San Francisco district attorney's office after clashes with Hallinan's assistant. Soon after, she joined city attorney Louise Renne at San Francisco City Hall.

2004 Elected as district attorney of San Francisco. She became the first person of colour to hold the post and continued in it for another term until 2011. In the same year, she created the San Francisco Reentry Division, launching the successful reform programme called Back on Track for first-time non-violent offenders aged 18 to 30.

2005 Founded the Environmental Crimes Unit. She was awarded the Thurgood Marshall Award by the National Black Prosecutors Association in recognition of her long-term contributions to the advancement of civil rights, civil liberties and human rights in the United States.

2008 Announced her candidature for the post of California's attorney general.

2009 Lost her mother to colon cancer.

2011 Sworn in on 3 January as the thirty-second attorney general of California. She became the first woman, the first African American and the first South Asian American in California's history to be elected to this post.

2012   Secured a multi-billion-dollar settlement for victims of illegal foreclosures from five of the biggest banks in the country.

2013   Introduced the Homeowner Bill of Rights to safeguard people against aggressive foreclosure measures. She also launched the California Department of Justice's Division of Recidivism Reduction and Re-Entry in partnership with district attorney offices in major Californian cities – San Diego, Los Angeles and Alameda County. She was named as one of the '100 Most Influential People in the World' by *Time* magazine.

2014   Re-elected as attorney general of California to serve a second term. She married attorney and entertainment litigator Doug Emhoff.

2015   Launched the reform programme Back on Track for first-time non-violent offenders aged 18 to 30 in Los Angeles. She also announced her candidature for the Senate the same year.

2016   Defeated her contender Loretta Sanchez for a position in the Senate, after being endorsed by President Barack Obama and Vice President Joe Biden. She was presented the Bipartisan Justice Award by the 20/20 Bipartisan Justice Center.

2017   Sworn into the Senate on 3 January by Vice President Joe Biden. Kamla emerged as a stern critic of the Trump administration that had just come into power. She also garnered a lot of attention and appreciation for the questioning of top Trump administration officials like Rod Rosenstein, the United States deputy attorney general, and Jeff Sessions, the United States attorney general, during hearings to confirm their posts.

2018   Became a target of the mail bombing attempts – sixteen packages with pipe bombs were delivered to various Democratic Party politicians and critics of the Trump administration via the United States Postal Service. She also announced her candidature for the 2020 presidential election.

2019   Served in the Senate as a member of several committees such as the Committee on the Budget, Committee on Homeland Security and Governmental Affairs, Select Committee on Intelligence, and Committee on the Judiciary. She also worked on her presidential campaign, going through highs and lows and ultimately withdrawing from the race at the end of the year.

2020   In March, she expressed her support for Joe Biden by endorsing him for President. Biden, who was looking for a running mate for his presidential campaign, announced her name for the position in August. She is the first African American, the first Indian American, and the third woman to get a vice presidential nomination. The two emerged as a winning team, defeating Donald Trump in the elections in November. They delivered their victory speeches on 7 November in Wilmington, Delaware.

2021   Assumed office as vice president of the United States of America on 20 January. She is the first African American, the first Indian American and first woman vice president of the United States in the history of the country.

REFERENCES

'Attorney General Kamala Harris honored for rape kit processing', CBS Sacramento, 8 April 2014.

'Full text of US Vice President-elect Kamala Harris' victory speech', *Indian Express*, 8 November 2020.

'Kashmiris are not alone in the world, says US presidential candidate', *Dawn*, 8 October 2019.

'Kamala Harris had an affair with a 60-year-old married man when she was 29 who "launched her career"', *Free Press Journal*, 13 August 2020.

'"Look Forward to Working Closely": PM Congratulates Joe Biden', NDTV, 8 November 2020.

Adam Edelman, 'The first "second gentleman"? Meet Kamala Harris' husband, Doug Emhoff', NBC News, 13 August 2020.

Alexei Koseff, 'Kamala Harris aide resigns after harassment, retaliation settlement surfaces', *Sacramento Bee*, 5 December 2018.

Anna Silman, 'How I get it done: Kamala Harris', *Cut*, 28 August 2018.

Barbara Parker and Rebecca Kaplan, 'Kamala Harris's foreclosure deal a win for state', SFGate, 5 March 2012.

Ben Terris, 'Who is Kamala Harris, really? Ask her sister Maya', *Washington Post*, 23 July 2019.

Berkeley Lovelace Jr, 'Where Kamala Harris stands on coronavirus masks, stimulus checks and other pandemic spending', CNBC, 12 August 2020.

Christopher Cadlego, '"Everyone is used to relatives that are doofuses": Kamala's sister breaks tradition', *Politico*, 6 July 2019.

Colbert I. King, 'Kamala Harris's HBCU experience prepares her to take on Trump', *Washington Post*, 13 August 2020.

Dan Morain, '2 more brown associates get well-paid posts: Government: The Speaker appoints his frequent companion and a longtime friend to state boards as his hold on his own powerful position wanes', *LA Times*, 29 November 1994.

Danielle Zoellner, 'Maya Harris: Who is Kamala's younger sister and why do people call her the next "Bobby Kennedy"', *Independent*, 13 August 2020.

David Martosko, '"Half my family's from Jamaica. Are you kidding me?" Stanford professor Donald Harris, her proud Jamaican father, was not pleased. He wrote in his blog that his deceased grandmothers and parents "must be turning in their graves"', *Daily Mail*, 20 February 2019.

Donald Harris, 'Reflections of a Jamaican Father', *Jamaica Global*, 18 August 2020.

Eric Lach, 'Kamala Harris at the Democratic debate: "I would like to speak on the issue of race"', *New Yorker*, 27 June 2019.

Eugene Scott, 'Kamala Harris's post-debate diss on Tulsi Gabbard's polling reveals something about her candidacy', *Washington Post*, 1 August 2019.

Hadley Freeman, 'More than a second gentleman: Why Doug Emhoff is Kamala Harris' secret weapon', *Guardian*, 21 November 2020.

Holly Honderich and Samanthi Dissanayake, 'Kamala Harris: The many identities of the first woman vice-president', BBC News, 8 November 2020.

Isabella Grullón Paz, 'Kamala Harris and Joe Biden clash on race and busing', *New York Times*, 27 June 2019.

Joanne Slater, 'As Kamala D. Harris breaks barriers, India and Jamaica celebrate', *Washington Post*, 7 November 2020.

Jonathan Martin, Astead W. Herndon and Alexander Burns, 'How Kamala Harris's campaign unraveled', *New York Times*, 30 November 2019.

Kamala Harris, 'Sen. Kamala Harris on being "Momala"', *Elle*, 10 May 2019.

Kamala Harris, *Smart on Crime: A Career Prosecutor's Plan to Make Us Safer*, Chronicle Books, 2009.

Kamala Harris, *The Truths We Hold: An American Journey*, Random House, 2019.

Kat Stafford, 'Kamala Harris' selection as VP resonates with Black women', *Washington Post*, 11 August 2020.

Katie Mettler, 'As a prosecutor, Kamala Harris's doggedness was praised. As a senator, she's deemed "hysterical"', *Washington Post*, 14 June 2017.

Kevin Sullivan, '"I am who I am": Kamala Harris, daughter of Indian and Jamaican immigrants, defines herself simply as "American"', *Washington Post*, 2 February 2019.

Lara Bazelon, 'Kamala Harris was not a "progressive prosecutor"', *New York Times*, 17 January 2019.

Lisa Bonos, 'Kamala Harris's marriage inspires so many of us still searching for our Dougs', *Washington Post*, 9 November 2020.

Lisa Bonos, 'The story of Kamala and Doug, a match made in Hollywood (literally)', *Washington Post*, 19 August 2020.

Manuel Roing-Forina, 'Doug Emhoff paused his career for his wife Kamala Harris's aspirations – and became the campaign's "secret weapon"', *Washington Post*, 27 October 2020.

Marilla Steuter-Martin, 'High school friends of Kamala Harris in Montreal applaud her victory', CBC News, 7 November 2020.

Matt Bradley and Bill O'Reilly, 'How Sen. Kamala Harris' Indian heritage and pioneering mother propelled her', NBC News, 20 August 2020.

Matt Viser, 'Joe Biden picks Kamala Harris as vice president', *Washington Post*, 11 August 2020.

Meagan Flynn, '"You owe them an apology": Gabbard's attack highlights Harris's complex death penalty records', *Washington Post*, 1 August 2019.

Peter Baker and Maggie Haberman, 'Trump, in interview, calls wall talks "waste of time" and dismisses investigations', *New York Times*, 31 January 2019.

Phil Willon, 'Kamala Harris breaks a colour barrier with her US Senate win', *LA Times*, 8 November 2016.

Philip Elliott, 'How Joe Biden's enduring grief for his son helped lead him to Kamala Harris', *Time*, 12 August 2020.

Shobha Warrier, 'My niece, the US Senator', Rediff.com, 11 November 2016.